PSYCHOLOGICALLY UNEMPLOYABLE

LIFE ON YOUR TERMS

D1531559

FINNEY COUNTY PUBLIC LIBRARY
605 E. Walnut
Garden City, KS 67846

PSYCHOLOGICALLY UNEMPLOYABLE

LIFE ON YOUR TERMS

BY JEFFERY COMBS

A PUBLICATION OF MORE HEART THAN TALENT PUBLISHING, INC.

ISBN: 0-9740924-2-8

More Heart Than Talent Publishing, Inc.

6507 Pacific Ave #329 - Stockton, CA 95207 USA
Toll Free: 800-208-2260 FAX: 209-467-3260

www.MoreHeartThanTalentPublishing.com

Cover design by FlowMotion, Inc.

Illustrations by Rob Hider

Copyright © 2005 Jeffery Combs
All Rights Reserved.

Printed in the United States of America

SAN: 255 -2639

FOREWORD

by Jerry Clark

Yes, I know what you are thinking... ***Psychologically Unemployable: Life on Your Terms*** must be a book for people that don't have the basic talent necessary to get and keep a decent job... No, not at all! Instead, the book you now hold in your hands is specifically designed for those who realize that the talent they possess is worth a lot more than a J.O.B. could ever pay them.

Based on statistics from the 2004 U.S. Census Bureau report provided by the United States government, approximately 87 percent of Americans will retire in poverty, achieving less than $11,418 per year. According to these statistics, less than 6 percent of people aged sixty-five years or older have annual retirement incomes that exceed $50,000. We're not talking about some third world country in these reports—we're talking about the United States of America.

This is where the author of this book, my good friend Jeffery Combs, comes in. Jeff believes that entrepreneurship and free enterprise provide the vehicle for people to create the financial freedom they seek to live life on their terms. He has personally mentored thousands of people just like you who have found that they are "psychologically unemployable"—they have discovered that the confines of a traditional job have not served them. These renegades who have the courage to challenge the system and build their own enterprises are the entrepreneurs of our society who have overcome their challenges and dysfunctions to become successful.

Speaking of dysfunction, Jeffery Combs believes that the greater the dysfunction has been in your life, the greater your chances of breaking out of the traditional "rat race" system and becoming massively successful. As a matter of fact, dysfunctions seem to be one of the hallmarks of the world's most successful *Psychologically Unemployable* multimillionaires.

That's right—Bill Gates, Oprah Winfrey, Steven Spielberg, Michael Dell, Steven Jobs, Martha Stewart, Richard Branson, and many more are all examples of people who are or once were *Psychologically Unemployable*.

Jeff also falls into this category. I believe the catalyst for Jeff to create a seven-figure income through his own seminar company that perpetuates year after year after year is the simple fact that from the very first day I met him in 1991, and even before that, he was *Psychologically Unemployable*. In this book, Jeff will give you his detailed explanation of what it means to be *Psychologically Unemployable* and how to use your talents to create skills that will allow you to live life on your terms as an entrepreneur.

I'm excited for you. Why? Because I've used the same principles, philosophies, strategies, and techniques that Jeff will be sharing with you to produce my own personal fortune after firing my boss in 1989 at the ripe age of 21. That's when I realized that I was infected with the *Psychologically Unemployable* "Thought Virus"—and it built up my "Mental Terrain" to the point of allowing me to enhance my "Entrepreneurial Immune System," which opened me up to learning and profiting from the same information Jeffery Combs is sharing with you.

Jeff is not only a sincere and passionate human being who on a daily basis walks his talk and practices what he preaches; he is also a "Freedom Fighter." If you let him, he will assist you in creating the mental transitions that are necessary to claim the freedom that you seek and deserve.

So, be sure to strap on your "Psychological Seat Belts"…

You are in for the ride of your life.

Go, Go, Go!!!

Jerry "DRhino" Clark
vwww.clubrhino.com

ACKNOWLEDGEMENTS

Several years ago, I desired to become an entrepreneur. After many ups and downs, challenges, and $80,000 worth of debt, I made a commitment to become an exceptional entrepreneur. It was at this point that I knew I was *Psychologically Unemployable* and could never go back "to that which did not serve me." This ride in free enterprise is a remarkable journey, and I am dedicating this book to all of you who have the courage to become who you are becoming. There is a special group of people who have assisted me in getting where I am today.

I thank my wife, Erica Combs, who is just as responsible as I am for bringing my ideas together to create this reality. I could not have done this project without her effort, creativity, patience, multitasking skills, and, most of all, her love. Her contribution is what makes us a great team.

I want to thank Christopher Mattock and his wife Jamie for their contributions—the cover design, book layout and artwork—and for all of their collaborations.

To Fredric Lehrman, my good friend: Thank you, Fred, for allowing me the quantum leaps through our many seminars together.

I want to thank my best friend and brother in free enterprise and life, Jerry Clark, for always being there with me and for me on the on the ride. Go, Go, Go, Jerry.

And most of all, I would like to thank my parents, Don and Judy Combs, for providing me with the courage, examples and genes to be who I am becoming!

CONTENTS

PART ONE   WHAT DOES IT MEAN TO BE
               PSYCHOLOGICALLY UNEMPLOYABLE?

Chapter 1   **Psychologically Unemployable**   **19**
Chapter 2   **Profile of an Entrepreneur**   **23**

               The Four L's
                 Love Self
                 Love People
                 Love Life
                 Love What You Do
               Your Attitude and Energy
               N.P.I.B.
               Create Opportunities
               Risk for Reward
               Eliminate Chaos
               Understand Perfection

PART TWO   THE BEGINNING, THE PROCESS,
               AND FIRST STEPS

Chapter 3   **Beliefs**   **37**

               Break Free of Limiting Beliefs
               General Beliefs
               Beliefs Are Self-Fulfilling
               Making the Change
               An Exceptional Example

Chapter 4 **Turning Challenges Into Triumphs** **47**

Faith
Attitude
Leadership
Listening
Enthusiasm About People
Enthusiasm About Fundamentals
Enthusiasm About the Learning Process
Be Enthusiastic Everywhere
Enthusiasm About Practice

Chapter 5 **Cultivating Faith** **59**

The Four-Letter Word
Change Is Inevitable
Healing through Faith
Heal Thyself

PART THREE DECIDING WHAT I WANT TO BE
WHEN I GROW UP

Chapter 6 **Your Abundance and Prosperity** **67**
Purpose

What Do You Want?
Self-Fulfillment in Your Own Business
Money and Prosperity Exercise
Ads to Yourself and the Universe

Chapter 7 **Getting Money Right: What You** **77**
Deserve

Beliefs About Money are Changing
Take Leadership
Changes You Can Make
Do What You Want to Do
Average Thinking Produces Average
Results

PART FOUR   THE SKILLS AND THE MINDSET

Chapter 8   **Consistency**   **93**

Losers Play to Avoid Loss
Contract for Goal Getting

Chapter 9   **Raise Your Deserve Quotient**   **99**

Resignation
Throwing It Away
Settling
Denial
The Fatal Flaw
Blaming
Poor, Poor, Pitiful Me
Poverty Consciousness
Change Is a Process

Chapter 10   **Attracting Quality People**   **109**

Where Do I Find Terrific People?
Keys to Attracting Quality
    People to Your Reality

Chapter 11   **Master the Art of Listening**   **117**

Toward Better Listening Filters
The Art of Conversation
Remembering Names
Men and Women Hear Different
    Things

Chapter 12   **Releasing Rejection**   **127**

Your Emotional Filing Cabinet
The Past Was Different High Achievers
Fear of Rejection Goes Beyond
    Business
Your Foundation of Rejection Is
    Ancient History
Really Not About You
Tools for Releasing Rejection

Part Five   Habits and Focus - Breaking It Down

Chapter 13   **What Is Success?**   **141**

Average People Operate from a
Position of Fear
What Precisely Do You Want to
Accomplish?
Success Myths - What Success Is
and Isn't
How It All Started for Me
Thirteen Qualities of Successful
People

Chapter 14   **Time – Your Most Valuable**   **147**
Commodity

The Paradox of Time Management
Turning Time Into Money Is a
Predictable Three Step Process
Setting Your Goals and Establishing
Your Whys
Find out How You Spend Your Time

Chapter 15   **Getting Unstuck – Breaking**   **159**
Through Barriers to Change

Why Change?
Psychological Myths About Change
Misperceptions About Change
A Matter of Will
What Is Resolve?

Chapter 16   **Goals vs. Results**   **169**

Self-Motivation
Action
Results

PART SIX   BECOMING - COMING INTO YOUR OWN
                  WITH CREATIVITY AND IDEAS

Chapter 17   **Inner Knowing -**   177
                  Using All Your Faculties for
                  Prosperity!

                  Join the Revolution
                  Change Your Focus

Chapter 18   **Identity - Defining Who You Are**   185

                  Who Are you?
                  Self Inventory
                  Redrawing Your Identity Map!
                  Make a Decision to Change and
                      Reinvent Your Identity
                  The Three Key Characteristics of Change

Chapter 19   **Get In the Game and Stay In the**   189
                  Game

                  Take a Chance and Participate
                  Participation Makes a Difference
                  Stay In the Game
                  Schedule for Results
                  Success Habits
                  Begin Creating Opportunities Instead
                      of Waiting for Them
                  Take Calculated Risks
                  Eliminate Chaos: Peace = Profit!
                  Become Proactive Instead of Reactive

Chapter 20   **Grow and Glow –**   199
                  What It Takes to Be a Winner

                  Living In the Now
                  The Importance of Focus
                  Don't Stop Here

PART ONE

WHAT DOES IT MEAN TO BE PSYCHOLOGICALLY UNEMPLOYABLE?

PSYCHOLOGICALLY UNEMPLOYABLE

What does it mean to be "psychologically unemployable"? Congratulations—if you are reading this book, your curiosity has been sparked by my title, and you are either already an entrepreneur or are in the process of becoming one. Psychologically unemployable means you are a renegade, an outcast, a throwback, a radical, a stallion, a mustang, a rebel, dysfunctional, don't fit in, out of the status quo, tired of trading time for dollars, an out-of-the-box thinker, an artist, a musician, or any multitude of other adjectives. The real point is that you are ready to achieve "more mores." This means more time on your terms to enjoy life and more opportunities to be creative in ways that will increase your value. This means more love, more peace, and many, many "more mores."

At the age of thirty-two, I realized that I would never get rich or wealthy working for someone else. I found, like you may have, that typical jobs pay what a job is worth and that the odds of getting rich and being able to express my true creativity in a job were minimal. I had always been creative and been a big thinker, but I had reached a level of consciousness that screamed "I can't do this!"—meaning work for someone else anymore.

I am the first son of two highly educated and creative parents. Although I had acquired a college degree and practical work skills, at this point I was going nowhere fast in life. Plain and simply, I wanted more in life. I wanted my dreams, I wanted to be creative, I wanted passion, I wanted purpose, I wanted to take off the tie, the shirt, and the penny loafers, I wanted to scream, "I want out!" and so I did. I eventually walked away from my job and ventured into "the land of the unknown," free enterprise. I was completely unprepared for that first step. I had no idea what it took to become an entrepreneur. I had dreamed of owning my own business. I had romanced and thought about the possibilities of being self-employed. But

I found very quickly that entrepreneurship required a different set of life skills then what I had learned operating in someone else's dream, otherwise known as a job. The first wave of feelings I felt was two-fold: I was exited and I was fearful. This situation is normal for any new entrepreneur. We all start at the same place, the beginning, when we decide to walk away from one career and begin our first venture. This is the place where most businesses never get off the ground, the idea stage.

The first step in being an entrepreneur is not so much the physical action of starting a business. It's about deciding, and this is what most people don't do. To succeed as an entrepreneur, you must decide to commit to a process that repeated over time will allow you to learn the skills required to master your new craft. As a society, we are impatient, and our expectations are extremely high. I believe we live in a commitment-phobic society where we are conditioned to live in fear and in debt. We may not like what we do for a living, but this situation our society has been conditioned to accept has also created a level of comfort that keeps most people from taking risks that will eventually bring them the rewards they deserve.

We are taught how to give, and we give, give, give, but seldom are we taught how to receive. "Better to give than receive" goes the old adage. Instead, I say it is great to do both. I believe receiving is intrinsically spiritual and is a skill that one must master to be a successful entrepreneur. This is why committing to the process is the most important step that you take. This means that you will get in the game and stay in the game to learn the life lessons that will allow you to create the value and perform the service that will eventually allow your enterprise to flourish. It takes courage to take that first step.

I have found that courage is a commodity that never goes out of fashion; there is always a market for it. Decide to have the courage to commit to the process, and decide that you have what it takes to create the success you desire.

You will find that not only will your decision be uncomfortable for you at times, but not everyone you know or love will automatically be in your corner. You will hear, "Grow up, get real, who do you think you are? You're a dreamer, stop dreaming, stop chasing rainbows, you're not smart enough, good enough," and a multitude of reasons why you can't, won't, shouldn't, couldn't, and will be unable to make it in your own business. Don't listen to them. Evaluate who is giving you this information. If it's the dogcatcher, the fireman, your next-door neighbor, or someone who is as broke as you are, reevaluate whom to listen to.

I Am Psychologically Unemployable!

This is why having a mentor or developing a mastermind team is important in the first stage of free enterprise. The average person is overwhelmed with "What to do?" This is the very reason that procrastination is so prevalent for the "want-to-be" success-seeker. The "getting ready to get ready" mentality is a great diversion and a great way to fool yourself into thinking that you are doing something when you are doing nothing. Surprisingly, this is a by product of you being so accustomed to having someone else tell you what to do. I feel that not only is success a process as an entrepreneur, but it is mostly about what you do daily. Your habits will make or break you.

It is so important to choose an endeavor or create a situational niche that you enjoy, because if you don't enjoy what you do, you will find every way possible to resist that which you are attempting to succeed at. We as humans operate from two perspectives in life: pleasure or pain. That which we perceive to be painful we resist, and that we perceive to be pleasurable we do. You see, this is the very reason that what you speak is exactly what you will get or receive. Your word is your law. As an entrepreneur, you are actually letting yourself have fun doing what you do versus "working really hard" or "trying to make myself do." These are work-related job and struggle-mentality type of statements that will not serve you. The time you spend worrying, pressuring yourself and stressing over how you are going to succeed will have an adverse effect.

Deep breathing will serve as a new anchor to allow yourself to let go when fear and anxiety enter your consciousness. When fear and anxiety knock on your door, learn to allow yourself a different level of breathing from your diaphragm rather than the anxious, pressure-based, performance-oriented, everyday job-type shallow breathing of stress. Learn to stay in your power by letting go and enjoying the process rather than making yourself do.

Profile of an Entrepreneur

What is the difference between ordinary and extraordinary, between average and exceptional, mediocre and superb? What is the difference between being an employee, a struggling business owner, and an exceptional entrepreneur? Most of us have had the opportunity to be an employee at some point in our lives, and many of us have discovered that we were psychologically unemployable. Many of us then found an opportunity to step away from Corporate America, out of a job and into free enterprise, starting our own businesses with the intention of beginning to live life on our terms, manifest our dreams, achieve wealth, stop struggling, and start enjoying the time we spend producing.

The challenge most of us encounter very early in the game is that we have no idea what successful entrepreneurs do. Most of us do not have entrepreneurial parents and have not spent time with successful entrepreneurs to see what they do, how they do what they do, who they spend time with, what books they read, what tapes they listen to, how they invest, how they create results, and how they achieve their goals. The good news is that there are more people seeking the opportunity to step into free enterprise each and every year. Most bookstores have entire sections devoted to self-help, motivation, business, money, and business motivation. This means that you do not have to personally know or meet exceptional entrepreneurs to learn from them. This means you can use the material you find in bookstores, such as the information in this book, to teach yourself and to find role models whose examples you can follow.

I have spent lots of time studying entrepreneurs during my journey. I have also had the privilege of spending time masterminding and collaborating with exceptional people like Mark Victor Hansen, Jim Rohn, Jerry Clark, Stephen Simon and other self-made millionaires as I have evolved and grown. Here is an entrepreneurial profile to assist you in

Creating Your Entrepreneurial Identity

understanding what separates the average from the exceptional so that you can begin to transform yourself, your enterprise, and your life.

The Four L's

Love Self

Successful entrepreneurs have great self-esteem. They truly love themselves and because of this, they are comfortable being who they are. They allow people to see who they are so that others have the opportunity to like them as well as to do business with them. When your clients and associates know that you feel good about yourself, they are naturally drawn to you, and when you allow them to know and like the real you, they will become lifetime connections.

Developing a great self-esteem is imperative in the journey of free enterprise, because while you are marketing your products and services you are also marketing yourself. Your uniqueness is what separates you from the competition. It is the value that only you can bring to the marketplace. When you can resonate from a position that says, "I am very comfortable with myself," you will notice that more people will want do business with you.

Love People

Every entrepreneur I have ever met has a great love for people. You require other people to purchase from you, and as your business grows, you will require a team of people to assist you in your endeavor. When you have an intrinsic love for people, you are able to see the intentions behind other people's actions, even if the results of their actions are less than desirable. You are able to assist people to grow and change, and you are able to enjoy the time you spend with them throughout the day. You will find very quickly that most people really don't care how much you know; they care about how much you care.

When other people feel how much you care about them and how much you enjoy their company, they will naturally be compelled to spend time with you and to conduct business with you. It is so much easier to build a business when you have lifelong clients referring you business than when you simply have customers who complete one transaction with you and then move on.

Love Life

Becoming an entrepreneur and living life on your terms is a process and a privilege. Producing revenue from the comfort of your own home, or the comfort of an office of your design, is a gift that only you can give yourself. Operating according to your own time clock and production schedule is a luxury to be enjoyed. Take time each day to be grateful for what you are creating. Enjoy the fruits of your labor. When you love your life and you love your enterprise, you will allow yourself to spend more time doing what you love.

You will create many decisions on your journey in free enterprise about how you spend your time, which friends you surround yourself with, who you mentor with, and the amount of time you are willing to dedicate to your enterprise to achieve your desired outcome. Each of these decisions will impact your success, and having the opportunity to make these decisions is a privilege, not a sacrifice. Love every second of every day because each one is a gift, and once they are gone, they are not retrievable.

Love What You Do

When you love what you have chosen as your vocation to create the freedom you deserve, you are truly designing your life. What you *do for a living* is not nearly as important as what you do *while you are living*. Choose an opportunity or create an enterprise that you love spending time in. Allow yourself to have so much fun that there is nothing else you would rather do. Allow yourself to be creative and use your talents so that they become skills. Hone your craft and love every second of the process!

When other people see you enjoying your enterprise, they will want to share the experience with you!

Does medicine have to taste bad to be good? Do you have to work really hard to produce results on your terms? Who said producing isn't fun? Begin to give yourself a new set of permissions to love your vocation, and I guarantee you will achieve a new level of results and success!

Your Attitude and Energy

Entrepreneurs have a special attitude; it is positive. When I say positive, I am not talking about being excited, jazzed, juiced, jacked, or pumped up. When I say positive, I mean they believe in the good in life and the good in people. They have an attitude and a mindset that expects good situations and good people to find them.

Entrepreneurs are perpetual optimists. This means having the ability to see a positive outcome or lesson in every situation. This is the glass half-full principle. A perpetual optimist does not believe in failure, but sees every experience as an opportunity to grow and change. Sometimes the outcome is exactly as desired and sometimes it is not. When it is not, the questions to ask are: "What can I learn from this? Who will I meet because of this? How can I grow from this experience? What will I do differently next time?" This is place where the old adage "turning lemons into lemonade" comes into play.

When you are able to remain positive in the face of adversity, as well as when the going is easy, you will begin to radiate a different kind of energy. This is called etheric energy, and it is the subconscious message each of us sends that other people intuitively feel. When you know that you are growing, changing, and becoming a better person for each experience you have as an entrepreneur, and when you begin to expect good situations and people to find you, you begin to emit a different kind of energy. Your subconscious message becomes "I am the leader people are looking for."

Our society is starving for leadership. Our society is seeking agents of change; i.e., people who are willing to act against the status quo to create a new and empowering reality. People are tired of being average and are drawn to those who have made the decision to become exceptional. When you have made this decision to be exceptional, to remain perpetually positive, to become a leader, to be different than what is accepted as "the norm," you will begin to attract better opportunities and situations to you. I believe that opportunities are never lost; they are always taken by the right people.

N.P.I.B.

Nothing Personal in Business. This is a powerful concept to understand, internalize, and implement. One of the keys to succeeding in free enterprise is becoming emotionally resilient. When you are emotionally resilient, nothing gets you down for very long, and nothing gets you so excited that you go in the tank if the outcome is less than perfect.

N.P.I.B. means that you begin to take yourself out of the equation; it means that you stop taking every situation and every decision personally. Sometimes it is necessary as an entrepreneur to create decisions in your business that have nothing to do with the person you are doing business with, because you are making the very best decision for your enterprise. The people you do business with will also find themselves in the same situations at times while conducting business with you. It is imperative that you realize that business really is business; it is not personal.

Understand that when I say this I am not implying that business transactions are not heartfelt. I am a firm believer that people do not care how much you know; they care how much you care. When you are able to be emotionally resilient, you will be able to establish and maintain great connections with other entrepreneurs, and these connections will remain solid, regardless of the business decisions you and your colleagues create. When you are able to be objective and to understand business decisions without internalizing them, you will begin to create a foundation for your enterprise that is unshakable.

Create Opportunities

The ability to create opportunity is a skill that every successful entrepreneur develops at some point in their journey. I call this "O.S.P – Opportunity Seeking Perception."

O.S.P. means that if opportunity is banging down your front door, you open your window and invite a new situation in. I cannot tell you how many times I have faced the proverbial "donut hole" (no money in the till) in my own enterprises and made the decision that I would not close out my day without a sale. These are the times when I go back through my contacts and clients and choose the person I will approach with my services and offer them the opportunity to hire me.

O.S.P. also means being open to the opportunity to risk for reward, meaning realizing that in a given situation, you have an opportunity to realize a situation where you can capitalize or gain from the result.

Risk for Reward

When you are able to consistently risk for reward, you will begin to receive more of the rewards you are seeking. Successful entrepreneurs are constantly seeking change in their lives and in their enterprises and are constantly taking calculated risks to achieve the rewards and results they desire.

Many people in our society will also risk for reward; however, most have a skewed view of reward versus risk. For instance, many people will take the risk of $5, $10, $100, or even $1,000 to win the lottery when the jackpot is 50 million dollars. This is taking a very small risk for a very large reward. The odds of achieving the desired result, winning the lottery, are miniscule.

The difference between average and exceptional entrepreneurs is that exceptional entrepreneurs are willing to consistently take calculated risks to achieve a desired outcome in a field where they understand the odds, and the odds are usually slightly in their favor to win. They also understand that there is the possibility that the risk may not return a reward, and so they do not risk their entire bank account on one situation. They also do not bank the future of their enterprise on one large transaction.

Exceptional entrepreneurs also understand that the greater the risk, usually the greater the reward. If you know that you would like to be able to take large risks with the possibility of receiving large returns, then the game becomes getting good at capitalizing on lots of opportunities that will yield a definite return so that you can also take larger risks without ending up severely in the hole if the result you were seeking does not manifest.

Eliminate Chaos

Second only to fear, chaos is the ultimate sabotage of many entrepreneurs. I have seen many people fall victim to their chaos, both internal and external, and have also seen many people learn to release their chaos to become victors in the entrepreneurial arena.

Chaos is quite simply a lack of order. Are you a neat freak? If so, you probably do not have much external chaos in your life. Your desk is organized; there is a place for everything and everything in its place. Your drawers and closets look as great on the inside as they do on the outside. The neatness is not for show; you are truly pleased with the order and systems for organization that you create, and you continue this habit for the sheer pleasure you derive from being neat.

However, if you are a chaos addict, your desk is piled with papers and notes, and seeing the top of it is often challenging. I have clients who actually cannot remember the color of their office carpet because the floor is covered in miscellaneous papers, magazines, faxes, and notes. When you open your desk drawers, you never quite know what you may find in them on any given day, and your closets are just as likely to have clothes piled in heaps as you are to have them hanging up on hangers. Even if you are able to organize your office on the surface, if you were to look beyond your desktop and drawer fronts, you would find a jumble of disorganized information and materials.

A neat freak and a chaos addict are polar opposites on the sliding scale of disorganization. Most of us lie somewhere between these two extremes. I have used the example of external chaos that almost everyone can envision to illustrate my point. What I have found in the many thousands of hours I have spent coaching my clients is that external chaos typically reflects internal and emotional chaos.

A key component to success as an entrepreneur is developing a crystal clear vision of where your enterprise is headed. If you are just realizing that you are surrounded by chaos, here are a few questions that will assist you: What is your purpose? What is your reason for being psychologically unemployable? What changes do you seek to create in the world through your endeavor? What people would you like to meet? What charities or organizations would you like to donate your time and money to? What destinations would you like to travel to? Questions like these will provoke you to create mental images of your entrepreneurial future.

Now take a look at your office, your entrepreneurial present. Is it as precise and clear as your visions? Does it in any way reflect your emotional state at this point in time? If the answer is yes and you do not like what you see, the good news is that when you are your own boss you can choose to hire and fire yourself every day! If you are in emotional turmoil in your enterprise, welcome to the big leagues! So is just about every other new entrepreneur stepping into this game. Begin by taking a few deep breaths and letting go of some of your anxiety. Take a look around you and commit to eliminating anything that no longer serves you. You will be amazed at the change you can create in your office in ten minutes when you allow yourself to release the chaos!

If you are at the opposite end of the spectrum and your office is as neat as a pin, I ask you to consider if you are spending in inordinate amount of time each day maintaining this order. If the answer is yes, then you may actually be procrastinating instead of taking the action that will produce results in your enterprise. Having a perfect office may be your way of convincing yourself that you put in a full day's effort, when really you took little action. If this is the case, ask yourself what it is that you are resisting in your enterprise. Then take a deep breath and begin letting go of this fear.

Perhaps, like me, you are extremely organized and spend little time or energy staying organized because this is in your nature and it is just how you are. If this is the case, you are in a very small percent of society, and this skill will be one of your greatest assets in free enterprise.

Regardless of where you stand on the chaos scale, there is always room for improvement—whether you seek to become more organized or to let go of your obsessive behavior to achieve more results. The key here is to find a balance that you can maintain with a minimum amount of effort and to have an office or production space that you are proud of and feels good to be in.

Understand Perfection

I touched on this concept briefly a moment ago, in the form of perfectionism actually being procrastination or what I call "unwarranted perfection." There are actually two kinds of perfectionism—practical and neurotic.

Practical perfectionists are people who pay attention to details. They take time to read their emails before clicking "Send" to check their grammar and spelling. Practical perfectionists realize that despite their best intentions, no one is ever perfect, and although they strive for excellence in all that they do, they are able to move on to new tasks and do not spend more time on any one situation than is merited.

Neurotic perfectionists, on the other hand, are so consumed with the idea of being perfect that they often become paralyzed by their imperfections before taking any action. Neurotic perfectionists generally assume all of the blame if a situation or opportunity does not pan out as intended, because they feel they did not take the correct action or say the right words. Neurotic perfectionists focus on, "When the time is right, I will _____." They spend so much time getting ready to get ready that they are never ready. This is what I refer to as procrastination, or unwarranted perfection.

Exceptional entrepreneurs recognize their strengths as well as their weaknesses, but they focus on their strengths. They realize that there is no such situation as saying the wrong words to the right people, and they move forward with presenting their ideas, products and services, regardless of the audience. They realize that there are times when perfection is appropriate, such as when offering a proposal or formulating a contract, but they also realize that the key to success is action, and they do not allow themselves to become paralyzed by everyday minutia.

PART TWO

THE BEGINNING, THE PROCESS, AND FIRST STEPS

BELIEFS

Webster's Dictionary defines *belief* as "a state or habit of mind in which trust or confidence is placed in some person or thing." In order to achieve success, you must believe you will be successful before you start. I know this sounds trite and like a cliché; nevertheless, it's very important and fundamental. Success is not achieved by thinking like a successful person after you become one. Success is achieved by having a millionaire mentality—meaning you think like a millionaire NOW, not after you become a millionaire. How will you become successful if you don't begin to see and think yourself successful? It's not possible. Your personal beliefs have created your life experiences to this point. This is the perfect time to begin addressing some of these beliefs.

Beliefs are the thoughts we adopt to rule our lives. Why is it that one man's gold is another man's junk? Why is it that when two people are faced with a challenge, one person sees certain failure while the other person sees adversity as a reason to succeed? Most people buy their own excuses and barely get by. They barely make a living, yet a few motivated and focused individuals become successful—not by getting by, but by designing a life. Most people are willing to believe that childhood and adult events have shaped their lives. Not true. It's not the events that shape our lives, but rather our perception and beliefs of those events that have the greatest impact.

Break Free of Limiting Beliefs

You have probably known or read about remarkable people who have suffered loss and abuse, but still prevailed and became triumphant survivors instead of beaten down victims. Think of the men who served in war situations and were captured, beaten, and tortured by their captors. Many chose to die or committed suicide; however, some of those same captives made the decision to believe in life and in the power of the human spirit. It is never the environment; it is never the events, but the meaning we attach to the events that matters. It is how we see, view, and interpret these events that shape who we are today and who we'll become tomorrow. Beliefs are what determine whether you play and win the game of life or sit on the bleachers of life and collect splinters. Beliefs are what separate the winners from the whiners and the champs from the chumps!

Our beliefs are the guiding force to tell us what will lead to pleasure and what will lead to pain. Whenever situations happen in our life, our brain has two questions: Will this bring pleasure or pain? What must I do to avoid pain or gain pleasure? The answers to these two questions are based on our beliefs. Our beliefs take the shape of generalizations about what we've learned that could lead to pleasure or pain. These generalizations guide all of our actions and thus the direction and quality of our lives.

Break Free of Limiting Beliefs

General Beliefs

Generalizations give us a sense of certainty about the tasks or jobs we perform, hence the term, "generally speaking." This refers to the routine, the almost certain, what is considered normal. Generally, our society is conditioned to get a job and get a paycheck every two weeks, and in most cases, there is more month left at the end of the money. Why do we believe this to be true? Because our experience of what we witnessed and participated in has provided enough references to create a sense of certainty that creates that expectation. Having a sense of certainty allows us to function and perform our day-to-day tasks such as driving a car, going to the mall, and depositing money into a checking or savings account.

Generalizations are also what create self-limiting beliefs in more intricate areas of our lives. Perhaps you have failed or been unsuccessful in other businesses in your life, and based on that experience, you have developed a belief or a fear that keeps you stuck. Perhaps you have heard these generalizations from other people when talking about having your own business:

- Sounds difficult.
- I tried that once. It didn't work for me.
- Sounds like you have to do sales work.
- Those types of businesses never work.
- You'll never make it with your lack of experience.
- Sounds like a scam to me.
- Get real! You're such a dreamer!
- Grow up!
- People like us are never successful in business.
- Don't invest any money!

I'm sure you can come up with many other generalizations for any endeavor you have ever attempted.

Beliefs Are Self-Fulfilling

Once you believe a statement to be true, it becomes a self-fulfilling prophecy. "Why even try?" or "I'll give it a shot, but it probably won't work," or "I'll give it my best effort" are all statements that really mean, "I don't believe I'll make it, but I'll go through the motions in case anybody asks whether I made an effort, but I know full well that I won't be successful at this anyway. At least I won't disappoint myself."

How many of you received poor grades in school and believed the generalization that you weren't bright or that you were a slow learner? These generalizations are perceptions based on our past and often the opinion of someone else. These very generalizations are what end up limiting us by narrowing our view of what we deserve.

Average people think very realistically, while successful people tend to think out of the box, or somewhat unrealistically. My whole point is that generalizations form our beliefs and therefore become limitations that we impose upon ourselves. Most of our beliefs are nothing more than generalizations of past experiences and misinterpretations of painful and pleasurable incidents.

Here are three challenges that each of us face regarding generalizations and beliefs:

1. Most of us do not create conscious decisions about what we will or won't believe.
2. Our beliefs are misinterpretations of past experiences.
3. Once we adopt a belief as our own, we tend to forget that it is merely an interpretation of a situation that can be reinterpreted at any time, and we accept it as a fact.

The challenges listed above are the very reasons that a large number of people fail when they get out of the box or out on their own in free enterprise. These people perceive that situations are more difficult than they are, or worse yet, they just do not see or believe themselves to be capable of success. Many times, people with this belief and thought process will go through the motions of attempting to achieve, but in reality, they continuously sabotage their success without ever understanding why.

Making the Change

Until we learn to change our thinking, we continue to treat our beliefs as if they are realities. Many of our beliefs are, in fact, adopted limitations handed down by our parents, spouses, supervisors, teachers or other people we perceived to be authority figures. I have assisted scores of my clients to adopt a new set of permissions—their own! Giving up limitations for permissions is the process I call "reinventing yourself." The majority of people rarely, if ever, question their beliefs. Changing how we think and changing how we view situations is what allows us to grow and change as individuals.

Each of us has the power to create or the ability to merely exist. We have the capability to take any experience of our lives and create a meaning that is either disempowering or a meaning that can literally empower us and other people and positively change lives, especially our own. Unfortunately, some people take the pain associated with their past and say, "Because of this, I will never be successful," and yet there are those who experience the same pain and choose another belief—a belief that says, "Because of this, I will assist others." These people say, "Because I'm an alcoholic and recovering drug addict, and because I've been abused, I will be in a better position to assist others to change their beliefs. I will now be in a situation to teach people about their potential as human beings."

I spent fourteen years of my life in addictions. I have spent the last sixteen years clean and sober. By reinventing my life and myself, I have been able to aid thousands of people with achieving the same transformations. We have all experienced challenges at different times in our lives. Some of you are challenged even as I write these words. In my early thirties, I had reached a point in my life where I had to change or my options were going to be very bleak. I made a decision to adopt a new philosophy of life. Over a period of time, I was able to pick up my shattered dreams and begin my process of transformation. I consciously decided to begin living an empowered life. It was a choice and as we all know, the choice is always there for us when we are ready to acknowledge it. Changing your long adopted, old, comfortable beliefs takes time. It's a process, not an overnight sensation. Look at the process of change as a marathon, not a sprint. You must be willing to go through the process in order to collect the payoff. It's time for you to recognize the capacity you have for change and literally become the person you know you deserve to be.

Never underestimate the power of your beliefs. Studies have shown that people who are ill and undergoing radical drug treatments must first believe the treatment will create a cure before it ever does. Your beliefs about losing weight, experiencing success or prosperity will ultimately be your determining factor.

Stop reading this information and take a moment to identify your belief about what you have just read. Some of you are saying, "Yes, this makes sense," and others are saying, "This is ridiculous, and I don't believe a word." My recommendation is that you take just a moment to question your own beliefs right now. Why do you believe what I'm suggesting to be true or not true? Is that *your* belief or a belief you've accepted from some other person? What might it cost you to change? What might you gain by changing?

A great way to understand a belief is to think about its foundation. A belief is simply an idea. There are many ideas you may think but not really believe. It all begins is with you. Do you love yourself? Stop reading for a second and say aloud, "I love myself." Now, whether that statement is an idea or a belief depends on the amount of certainty you feel about this phrase as you speak it out loud. If you think, "Well, I do love myself most of the time," what you are really saying is, "I don't feel certain that I do love myself." If you do not love yourself, it will be very difficult for you to maintain your self-confidence. When self-love is not present, it is nearly impossible to attract and receive love and to give love to others.

- What beliefs do you now have that are empowering to you regarding success?
- What beliefs do you now know are disempowering to you and your quest for success?
- Are most of your current beliefs moving you forward or holding you back from achieving success?

Every great achiever has had the ability to feel certain they could succeed, even though no one before them had ever accomplished what they had set out to do. Successful people have beliefs that are not average. They may say, "Hey, the cards are stacked against me, but I know I can do it anyway." These people become successful because they believed they would beforehand! Successful people persist even when other people, including family, friends, and business associates, all told them they were crazy to even try! If you wait for the result you want before you change your thinking, you will have a very long (and perhaps painful) wait.

An Exceptional Example

I have a very good friend, Jerry Clark. He's a successful motivational speaker. I have had the privilege of knowing Jerry since 1991. Jerry answered a newspaper ad that I ran in the Oakland Tribune. I ran an ad and I received over 400 phone calls in about a two-week period. No one saw the value in my business. The exception was Jerry Clark. Jerry was born in a garage in Mississippi—not a great situation. Jerry didn't know his father until many years later in his life, and he was raised by a single mother in the housing projects in Pittsburg, California. Jerry was able to put himself through college by holding two or three jobs at a time in high school.

Jerry had a dream by the time he was eighteen or nineteen years old. He dreamed of becoming a motivational speaker. He realized that his ticket through the door on that journey was network marketing. By the time Jerry was twenty-five years old, he started the transition to become to a successful motivational speaker. I had the privilege of watching Jerry go through this whole process. He produced his first tape series in his bedroom on a little analog tape machine. Even though it wasn't perfect, he still had it out in the market, and that became his signature product. By the time Jerry was twenty-eight years old, he had reached the status of millionaire.

It's a good thing Jerry didn't listen to what everyone told him, saying, "You'll never get out of the projects. People like us never succeed. See, Jerry, the deck's stacked against you. You better just get a job."

In my own situation, no one ever believed in me except me. There were times when I was certainly tested, sometimes nearly beyond my endurance, but I held fast to my beliefs of success. All of my family and friends used to tell me I was crazy. They told me to get a "real job" and to stop messing around with my goofy entrepreneurial endeavors. I always believed I would be successful, although I didn't know how. I realized early on that if someone were going to believe in me, it would be me first! I obviously wasn't going to get the support of family or friends because their beliefs about success were so limiting.

People often develop limiting beliefs about who they are and what they're capable of because they haven't succeeded in the past. They believe that because they didn't see success in the past, they're destined to have an unsuccessful future. I have learned that the past does not equal the future. Have you ever heard someone say to you, "Why don't you be more realistic?" Perhaps you have been told to get real about your goals or dreams. The people who are telling you these things are (in most cases) living in fear. They are afraid of being disappointed, so they don't bother to try the unknown or attempt something new. Out of this fear, they develop beliefs that cause them to hold back, be skeptical, think it over, or do endless research in order to avoid making a decision.

Here is the bottom line: think unrealistically. Turn your ideas into beliefs that serve your progress. Don't listen to other people unless they have obtained the success you are seeking. Other people may predict what you will or won't accomplish, but only you can determine your future!

TURNING CHALLENGES INTO TRIUMPHS

This chapter focuses on the main differences between people who achieve success and people who don't. Basically, what is the key component of people who live life to the fullest and fulfill themselves spiritually, physically and mentally? How do these people differ from the folks who settle for mediocre or even below average lives?

What makes great people great? How do top producers, leaders, and top income earners soar while others nest in the trees, watching and wishing for success? What separates the winners from the wishers? What exactly is it that allows a small percentage of people to achieve their goals while the largest percentage of our population sets goals but doesn't get goals?

As I speak, write, produce new training material, and mentor people who seek success and personal development, I am often asked why I do what I do. The answer is quite simple: I do what I do to assist people with change. I assist people seeking change that will allow them to think differently about the persons they are, where they have been, and what they are becoming. I use a saying quite frequently: "It doesn't matter where you start but how you finish." Great quote, don't you think? I don't know who said it first, but it's so apropos to achieving success. This decision to place myself in a position to assist people with positive change is what adds value to both their lives and mine as well. I love to teach, and it's very rewarding to assist people to achieve more and to become more.

In the game of life, success or failure is up to you. I feel pity for people who are so caught up in making a living that they never slow down long enough to realize they could achieve their dreams by focusing on designing a life. Nothing within the realm of the probable (most say possible) can stop the man or woman who is intelligently and ethically bent on success! Every person carries within them the key that unlocks either the front door of success or the rear door of failure. It is a matter of choice; which do you choose? I have interviewed thousands of people, and the vast majority has told me they strongly desire success. I set out to discover why so few attain it.

The road to success is paved with several key ingredients. These ingredients are characteristics that every person possesses and that exceptional entrepreneurs focus on developing into strengths.

Faith

Faith is a faculty of the mind. The person who has faith in his or her own ability accomplishes far more that the one who has no confidence in himself. Those who have great faith have great power. Strengthening your self-esteem is paramount to developing a strong faith in yourself. In order to have faith, you must have a conviction that all is well. In order to keep faith, you must allow nothing to enter your thoughts that will weaken this conviction. Faith is built from belief, acceptance, and trust. Your mind must be steady in its conviction that you have the ability to change; everyone does. This comes down to the desire to turn fear into faith. I did it and so can you.

Sixteen years ago, I was drinking a gallon of vodka a day. That tells you where my self-esteem was at that point in my life. My greatest fear then was that I couldn't stop drinking. I was actually at a point of not wanting to live any longer. I was living in fear. I thoroughly believe I experienced this pain and recovered from my addiction for a higher calling. It took a lot of personal growth to overcome my own fears. It all started with me getting okay with me, and that is where it starts with you. Just like success, faith is an inside job.

Men and women who live in faith have the opportunity and presence of mind to become successful. Those who live in fear or who are afraid to risk usually live and die in a struggle mentality, only wishing they could have acted more on their dreams. Faith is never passive; it must be active.

It is not simply theoretical acquiescence; it is positive cooperation. Faith is not just asking; faith means believing that you deserve what you ask for, and living as if you have already received in abundance what you ask for. Faith involves the launching of conscience and heart and will in the direction of what you desire.

Attitude

How do you feel about yourself? How do you feel about life? Do you view life as a struggle, or do you pursue life with gusto? Do you view your life as a successful one, or a life filled with failures? Success is an experience, as I stated before; it is an attitude. We are each voyagers on this quest called life. We ultimately arrive and depart alone. There is a great quote by the brilliant author, Stanley Bremer. He states, "There is no surer way along the road to success than to follow in the footsteps of those who have reached it."

Leadership

The ability to influence—have you developed this characteristic yet? Life, especially in our current business world, is about leadership. Are you the leader people are looking for?

Listening

Are you a good listener? Is this a skill you are developing? Do you really listen when others speak, or are you focused on what you will say next? Do you interrupt people mid-sentence?

Creating strengths from these key ingredients is the main difference between people who achieve and people who live average or less than average lives. The mighty eagle with its large wings cannot be confined to a barnyard, yet the vast majority of people dreaming of great heights of success wonder why they are left in the rear in the great race of life. Don't you think it's sad that students graduate from high school and universities never having been taught true success principles?

A hundred years ago, the dictionaries described uranium as a "rare, white, metallic substance with few known uses." During the past century, we have seen a power from this uranium that has changed the course of civilization. Virtually unlimited power existed forever in this relatively unknown substance, but since the power was unknown, it was unused. People are a lot like uranium. They are capable of tremendous accomplishments, but 99 out of 100 are content to drift aimlessly in the sea of life with no sails and no rudders, hoping to find land by accident. The reality of this situation is no map, no sails, no rudder, and therefore no land. To them, life is a struggle. They do not know their potential. They never learn to succeed. Only a small percent of their brilliance is ever tapped.

Talent on its own will never make you successful. The world is filled with talented people who never reach their potential. Potential is a word with a great amount of meaning, but when not used properly, potential is simply meaningless. The world is filled with talented people who never achieve greatness, and the world is also filled with average people who could be great and be great contributors, but aren't for one reason or another. Ultimately, your success will be determined by your attitude and the action you take over a long period of time.

Action must be consistent, not sporadic. The biggest mistake I see most people engage is lack of action. Most people are attached to the results, fear of failure, fear of success, fear of responsibility, fear of action, and fear of the unknown, and this keeps them paralyzed in their past. Many people don't like their past, but they continue to live there simply because it's not uncomfortable enough for them to change, even though change could benefit them.

Progress is made through change. The challenge of change is the fear that often accompanies it. Uncertainty and doubt can function like brakes to slow your acceleration toward personal growth. Vibrant learning with enthusiasm can transform uncertainty into activating curiosity as you continue to improve. It is a must that you believe you are successful or in the process of becoming successful. The road on the journey to success is filled with potholes and apparent dead ends. Some appear insurmountable at times. Many situations you will not be able to change. However, you can definitely change how you view the challenges. If you begin to look at each new challenge as a new learning experience, and are enthusiastic to be in the process, then you can also learn to transmute your positive energy and enthusiasm toward each encounter you experience every day.

Take aim at five primary targets for your ever-present enthusiasm. These are people (we are in the people business); fundamentals (learn the principles of success and enthusiasm); the learning process; be enthusiastic everywhere; and practice consistently until your enthusiasm becomes second nature.

Enthusiasm About People

Your enthusiasm must be infectious. People are much more impressed with your enthusiasm than they are with your knowledge. They don't care what you know. They care how much you care. Your enthusiasm rubs off on everyone you contact. You communicate your enthusiasm through your words, your voice quality and your body language. Would you want to be led by you? Ask yourself that question. Perhaps no other leadership quality is more important to building a team and becoming successful than true enthusiasm about people. You automatically seek and find the best in others, their qualities, virtues, and their potentials. Your enthusiasm acts like a magnet to draw these qualities out, assisting others to build their confidence and self-esteem.

I once read a great quote from basketball coaching legend John Wooden of UCLA, talking about leadership and team success: "It's amazing what is accomplished when no one cares who gets the credit."

Enthusiasm About Fundamentals

The fundamentals of success are the little things that produce the big results. These are the routines that aren't glamorous, but that done over a long period of time dramatically improve and enhance your results. Prospecting consistently—collecting decisions, listening, learning, reading, and becoming a student of the game—practiced consistently over a long period of time will allow you develop the skills that will ultimately produce the results you seek. The most successful leaders emphasize fundamentals above all else in their practical routines. The challenge for leaders when it comes to fundamentals is keeping themselves and their team focused. Most people want to move on to more glamorous or complex challenges rather than continually applying themselves to the basics.

People contact me on a weekly basis, saying they want to become a speaker, a trainer, or a motivational writer. This is great, but I find it alarming that almost all of these people are struggling in their various businesses. I always ask them, "How can you train and how can you motivate on what you yourself have not accomplished?" I paid eight years of dues figuring out the principles of success before I ever achieved any great levels of success. It took another two years before I felt I had enough life lessons and abilities to transmute what I had been through to teach it to the masses. Life is about collecting enough life lessons so that we can teach and pass on what was effective for us. We are all teachers at different points of our lives, and the better we become at our own success, the easier it is to teach it to others or to our teammates. That is why great leaders never ask anyone to do what they haven't done.

Enthusiasm About the Learning Process

This means developing an inherent enthusiasm for learning, growing, developing, and becoming the best you can possibly be. Progress is made through the evolution of change. A vibrant enthusiasm about learning can transform uncertainty into faith. If you desire to improve where you are, no quality is more important to instill than an enthusiasm for change fostered through personal growth and development. The very cultivation of thirst for knowledge fosters healthy habits to discover more and to become more, rather than living in fear and having to be right. Most often the greatest obstacle to learning the truth is the belief that you already know it all.

Over a period of time filled with many trials and tribulations, I finally got to a point where I learned I no longer had to be right all of the time. I spent the first thirty-nine years of my life with the philosophy that I was going to prove to everyone on the planet that I was right. I had a very low bank account balance with that philosophy. I now live the motto: "You be right, I'll be rich." I had a very humbling experience early in my entrepreneurial career when I abrasively approached a very successful woman involved in network marketing. I will never forget her exact words to me that my biggest problem was that "Your ego is bigger than your bank account," and that she would not collaborate with someone with my kind of attitude. This was the first of many turning points in my development. What she said really hit home with me. I didn't like what she said, but it forced me to look at who I was at that point in my life. My question to you is, "Is your ego bigger than your bank account?" If so, are you willing to create some changes so you can become a leader, a teacher, and a role model for other people? It is essential to adopt the belief that people collaborate with you as a leader, not for you. Success comes when you and other members of your team personally take ownership of the vision of success. This includes accepting responsibility for everyone's part in achieving goals. Often the best teachers of success are those you lead and serve. They become the agents who apply the principles and skills you teach. Their feedback and results are invaluable in enhancing your approach to success.

The greater the enthusiasm felt by the team, the greater the action, and the greater the momentum, because the team is motivated by desire rather than fear. Enthusiastic leadership can be expressed in many forms and varieties. It doesn't have to be loud and flashy. It requires only that you, the leader, express enthusiasm through some form of consistent action.

The successful entrepreneur is someone who never plays short-term. He or she is always thinking long-term. There have been many people I partnered with for no financial gain at the time. I assisted them regardless of whether they were in my company, my organization, my team, or even in the same industry as I was. Many of these people have since purchased my products, attended my seminars, hired me as a personal success coach, and referred me to many, many customers. Your goal is to become a great connector in life, not just in your present enterprise. Entrepreneurship is about connecting on many levels; it is about relationship and camaraderie. I refer to what we do as relationship marketing. You are looking for like-minded individuals you can partner with.

Be Enthusiastic Everywhere

Open your mind to the endless possibilities and locations to promote yourself, your products, your services, your company, and your leadership. Learn to love this part! My good friend, Jerry Clark, and I have both said that there are times when we speak and perform for free because we love what we do. We love the process—the process of becoming successful. Jerry started this process over thirteen years ago, and this year he is on track to gross well over one million dollars. Anywhere there is another human being, there is an opportunity. Do you hear the knocks, or are you afraid to open the door (the door of the unknown)? There is always the opportunity to connect in free enterprise. Here are just a few locations:

- Churches
- 12-step meetings
- Bookstores – self-help, business, personal growth sections
- Coffeehouses
- Parking lots (flyers on cars)

- Airports
- Airplanes (Ask "What do you do for a living?")
- Three-foot rule (Say "You look like someone who deserves this card.")
- Health clubs
- Real estate agents, insurance agents, doctors, lawyers, dentists, chiropractors
- Holistic health practitioners
- Health food stores (leave business cards and flyers)
- Reunions
- Health fairs
- Trade shows
- Kiosks in malls
- Roadside signs
- Newspapers
- Magazines
- Business cards in books
- Sporting events
- Consultants doing home sales presentations

These are just a few of hundreds of ways to find good people in the right places. When you become your own best publicist, this is when you will receive the most publicity, especially when you are just getting started in your own enterprise. Allow yourself to get creative. It is not so important to focus on the methods you use to create great connections; it is much more important that you create a process that you enjoy doing, so that you allow yourself to do lots of it!

Enthusiasm About Practice

Here I am referring to the practice required to excel at your craft. Like anything else, marketing, networking, and connecting are processes that can be learned but must be practiced to get them right. Always create a good first impression. You only have one chance to create the first impression. Isn't it logical to develop the skills that will accomplish this task? Here are some simple guidelines:

- Keep your business cards with you at all times in an easy and accessible place – don't be afraid to give them to people.
- Use your standard company business cards (and I suggest you always include your picture on the card), but have at least one more card that you use to attract attention. I call this a "curiosity card," because the purpose of this card is to create curiosity in the person you hand it to. I used to use a card that said "Frightened of being successful – let me scare you to death." Now I use a card that looks like this:

I simply say, "You look like someone who deserves this,"—simple, but very effective. This allows me to say less to more people so that I can promote myself more efficiently. My objective is simply to create enough curiosity to provoke a new contact to ask me what I do and then to look at my website or call my toll free number.

Develop an attitude of curiosity; begin to ask people, "Tell me about yourself." This is a short phrase that allows people to open up to you so that you have the opportunity to respond professionally and in a way that will attract interest and lead you into meaningful conversations. In person, don't get into a long sales presentation. Your goal is to create interest and curiosity. Get their business card, and take the time to look at it for a moment or two before resuming your conversation. This lets the other person know that you have a sincere interest in them and what they have to offer. Remember the three-foot rule: Anyone within three feet (about the length of a handshake) is a prospect and a possible contact.

Always smile and carry yourself like you are successful. "Fake it until you make it" if necessary. Successful people carry a positive energy and naturally attract the attention and interest of the people around them. People with a great self-esteem create this environment as well. They send an unconscious message that says, "I have value and I am very comfortable with myself," and this compels people to seek contact with them.

Have fun and take success and your enterprise seriously, but don't be too serious and don't fear the process. Remember that every "NO" is a temporary obstacle and not a permanent indictment. Don't get attached and don't take it personally. It's not about you, it's about them buying their excuses, or the timing just isn't right. Move on, let go, and go out and find the right people to collaborate with you! One of the easiest ways to attract these people to you is by becoming one of the people you seek yourself.

Entrepreneurial success is an attitude—both yours and the people around you. Your job is to allow others to see you as someone who really projects visionary, heartfelt leadership. Once you start to master this attitude, everyone you add to your contact list will have been touched by you in one way or another.

Remember, your task is to present, not convince; to sort, not sell. Proper marketing, networking, and connecting are definite win-win relationships.

Turning Challenges Into Triumphs

CULTIVATING FAITH

Daily thinking often falls into habitual patterns with little variation at all. People's lives mirror this serial monotony, interrupted by episodes of trouble, panic, and loss. Fear, lack, and poverty consciousness dominate such a life. Pretty soon life becomes a struggle. This is living in fear! The opposite of fear is faith. Faith is a science of the mind that takes seriously the assertion of being recreated through a complete renewing of your mind. And it's not only recreating your mind, but your body and soul as well. The opportunity to experience true abundance lies within you, but for this to occur you must agree to attune and orchestrate your thoughts and emotions toward higher purposes and creative ends. You are limited only by your own thought processes. You have been programmed by the thoughts of your grandparents, parents, peers, society as a whole, the media, the government, schools where a job mentality is learned, and, most of all, by you.

Having total faith in yourself and your outcome gives you the passion for a whole new probability, along with precise and clear directions for building a new consciousness that shouts, "I love myself; I deserve to have it all." Having faith allows you the opportunity to be active and creative.

The Four-Letter Word

It amazes me how many people I personally know and how many of my clients are paralyzed by the four-letter word FEAR. You have heard the clichés: "Fear stands for False Evidence Appearing Real," or "Fear will always be the thief of your dreams." Yes, fear creates paralyses. It stops many women and men from ever getting off the couch. I hear statements like, "If only," or "I'd like to," or "Next week," or "Next month," or "Next year," or how about "Next lifetime." Other versions include, "I'm not smart enough," or "old enough," or "wealthy enough." Such rationalizations are excuses that justify failure or the inaction that guarantees it. Fear causes people to avoid action that may bring ridicule or embarrassment. Many people fear success and the responsibilities they believe it will bring. A large portion of society has been conditioned through what is generally accepted as "work" into a comfort zone that is really the miserable comfort zone.

It takes as much or even more energy to be fearful as it does to have total faith. Look back on the amount of time and effort you have put into situations that you blew out of proportion. I call this majoring in minor things. Such over-dramatizations are examples of fear trumping faith. I spent the first 40 years of my life stressing, projecting, and worrying about the what-ifs of life. In the last few years, "This too shall pass" has become an affirmation I now use almost daily.

There is no space for fear when you have 100% faith to become successful in whatever job, business, or enterprise you undertake. If you fear you will fail, you are absolutely correct. If you are merely going to try, merely going to give it a shot, or merely interested or curious, then don't even bother getting started. Success is a process, not a payoff; you require action to become successful, and taking action requires risk. You will meet challenges and have trying moments. You will not be able to avoid some of the challenges, but you can definitely change how you view situations in the future. Turn fear into faith. Fear and faith do not mix. One percent doubt does not equal 100% faith. You can't have a little doubt and a lot of faith at the same time. You are either in fear or in faith—this is the choice you have.

Change Is Inevitable

Life is changing at an ever-quickening pace. Job losses in today's economy challenge the long-held belief that a job offers the possibility of financial security. These changes threaten us and offer opportunities that beckon us. Faith in who you are and where you are going is a major key to your peace of mind and to how successful you will be in any endeavor you undertake. We see abundance all around us in the universe. We cannot count the grains of sand on a single beach. Our universe contains untold riches. There is absolutely no reason that each one of us does not deserve to have it all. God does not play tricks on only you. The air is vibrant with power; the street really is paved with gold. Why do so few people ever live their dreams, achieve their goals, and find true abundance and prosperity? Why is the largest portion of our society stuck in mediocrity? Because they don't believe in themselves; fear has them paralyzed.

Faith has been recognized as a power throughout the ages whether it is faith in God, faith in one's fellowman, faith in oneself, or faith in a cause. Most people see faith in their religion. Faith is a faculty of the mind, and the man who has faith in his own ability accomplishes far more than the one who has no confidence in himself. Those who have great faith have great power. Why is it that one man's prayers are answered while another's remain unanswered? It cannot be that God desires better for one person than another. It must be that the different results are accounted for by differing individual beliefs. Faith is the affirmative mental approach to reality.

What is fear? It is nothing more than the negative use of faith—faith misplaced. The fear of lack is nothing more than the belief that the universe will not supply your desires. The fear of death is the belief that the promises of eternal life may not be true. We magnetize into our reality the thought processes that we think. This universal law manifests in both fear and faith. You must understand the power of your thought, the power of your mind, and what it can and will create. This is why it is so imperative that you are careful about what you speak and think. When your fear overcomes your faith and you project lack or speak into existence thoughts that are negative, they are bound to happen.

The brain operates as a transmitter and a receiver. This is the exact reason why when you think about someone, a few days later they call you.

There are no accidents. This is a synchronistic event. This is why I teach my clients to write down thirty-one qualities they seek in new prospects, job situations, mates, or opportunities. I am talking about magnetizing to your reality situations you desire. The Bible states that faith the size of a mustard seed will move a mountain.

We desire a faith based on the knowledge that there is nothing to fear! Faith is the substance of things desired, with the evidence not yet seen. The thought of faith molds the undifferentiated substance, and brings into manifestation the idea that was fashioned in the mind. This is how faith brings your desires to pass. When you use your creative imagination in strong faith, it creates for you out of the one substance whatever you have formed in thought. There is no end to the abundance life has to offer. This is why we require a strong faith in ourselves, in our spiritual side, and in new realities we will create and manifest. This is not a difficult task, but a thrilling opportunity to change our destinies. What a life this can be for you, if you will only step out of the dark and into the light! Why do you choose to live a life so hard and such a challenge?

Healing through Faith

History has recorded many instances of healing through faith. Such events have been documented in thousands of cases. Prayer has proven to be one of the strongest forms of faith and is definitely effective. Prayer is not an end in itself; it is a means to an end. Belief in self, faith in self, trust in self, and trusting your intuition are other key components to assist you in your quest for internal peace. This leap of faith often occurs just before you start to produce external results.

We've heard the sayings, "When fear creeps in" or "The only thing to fear is fear itself" from our Great Depression. Many of us let this kind of thinking seep deeply into our subconscious. Most people with low self-esteem and addictive behaviors live in fear-based or subconscious programming. Many independent businesspeople fear rejection and take it far too personally. This kind of thinking keeps many of us from operating on the faith side of the page. Fear of rejection keeps many people from even picking up the telephone. Understand that collecting "nos" is a major part of the process and is necessary for you to collect any "yeses." It is not personal. "Nos" are not an attack on you or your credibility. The more "nos" you collect, the faster you get to the "yeses."

Improving your self-esteem is essential to developing a strong faith in yourself. Faith is built from belief, acceptance, and trust. Developing a great self-esteem begins with believing that you have the ability to live your dreams and that regardless of your past history you deserve to receive all the good in life you desire. You have the ability to change; everyone does. Change becomes easier as you transform your fear into faith. I did it; so can you. Sixteen years ago I was drinking a gallon of vodka a day. That tells you where my self-esteem was at that point in my life. My greatest fear then was that I couldn't stop drinking. I was actually at a point of not wanting to live any longer. I was living in fear. I thoroughly believed I was spared this pain for a higher calling. It took a lot of growing to overcome my own fears. It all started with me getting OK with me and that is where it starts with you. Just like success; faith is an inside job.

Heal Thyself

Many people I meet want to assist and develop others. This is a great and noble idea. First and foremost, you must develop yourself. This is not selfish. It's hard to assist the poor when you are one of them. It is easy when you are prosperous. Your thoughts must be organized into positive affirmations for the purpose of vitalizing faith—for the purpose of converting thought to a belief in things spiritual. You must keep your faith vital if you are to successfully develop yourself and others—faith in the outcome you desire, faith that you will win, will succeed, and will overcome challenges and obstacles. The principles are invisible, and the laws must be accepted on faith. You must have complete faith in yourself, but also in your approach to becoming successful. You must know that you know!

Pure faith is a spiritual condition; it is the science of the mind—the embodiment of an idea put into action with 100% conviction that the idea and plan will create the desired outcome. This attitude shouts, "I will not be denied—I will claim it—victory is mine!" There are times that the desire is so great that a physical force comes over you and beats fear out of the door. When this happens you know that the truth you believe is stronger than the condition you are changing. Speak into existence the condition you will create. Follow with 100% faith and action, and it will be yours. This is why I always say, "Done, finished, completed!"

You deserve to operate in a state of relaxation (the hands free zone), not a state of fear and confusion. You deserve to operate in a state of poise, peace, and confidence—a state of spiritual understanding. By spiritual, I don't mean anything strange or supernatural, but merely a belief that goodness must be greater than any apparent manifestation of its opposite. It is this science of faith we are seeking to uncover—a definite technique that will conduct our minds through a process of thought that sublime minds of all ages have reached through direct intuition.

People suffer and struggle because they are not in both conscious and subjective communication with the affirmative side of the universe. All human struggles are a result of fear, and nothing but knowledge can free us from fear and its effects. Fear is a state of mind that many people adopt from their past failures, mistakes, and programming. It is time now—this is a call to action to let go of this four-letter bondage of FEAR and move into the higher state of consciousness called faith. It all starts with you—trusting in yourself, loving yourself, feeling good about you—knowing you have a purpose and finding that purpose. Trust yourself—you decide what you deserve—and you deserve to have it all!

PART THREE

DECIDING WHAT I WANT TO BE WHEN I GROW UP

Releasing Your Past Identity

YOUR ABUNDANCE AND PROSPERITY PURPOSE

What is human purpose? It is about growth, love, connecting, and your why. That's great! Now, how do you personalize it? What unique talents, assets, and perspectives can you offer? What is your purpose; what do you really feel passionate about? What is your calling? I'm sure you have all heard, "Do what you love and the money will follow." This is so true. If you are not pursuing a vocation, job or entrepreneurial endeavor that you truly love, rarely will you be paid what you are worth. What I am talking about here is "being purpose-driven to prosperity."

Have you ever wondered why some people are able to make their dreams a reality, while for the largest percent of society dreams remain only a fairy tale? What is that key ingredient that propels some people to the higher levels of prosperity, while others only wish? What is the difference between the few that make it happen and the majorities that watch it happen?

I have seen thousands of people attend seminars, rallies, conventions, and workshops. These people are pumped up, excited, jazzed, revved up, ready to explode, and they can't wait to get home and tear into their work. They experienced temporary motivation that existed for a flashing, fleeting moment and was gone very quickly. As the days wear on, the memories of the motivation seem to fade, and these people are right back where they were. People require much more than a temporary solution to get motivated to take consistent action over a long period of time. The real answer is that success is driven by inspiration, and your inspiration must be purpose-driven with a why and a how to live a prosperous life.

Motivation (and by this I mean self-motivation) is the natural by-product of inspiration. When you are inspired, you are on a real quest, and you are going to your promised land. Your life changes when you know you are in the right game. Most people spend their entire lives trying to find the right game instead of winning the game of their lives. If you knew that tomorrow you were leaving for an all expenses paid trip to the French Riviera for two weeks, you would probably feel great, no matter what other challenges you were facing. The challenges would simply be steps to take to get past today and into the morning. You probably wouldn't even mind you had to get up at 5:00 a.m. to catch your flight and then flying twenty-four hours to get to the Riviera. In fact, you probably wouldn't be able to sleep at all. You would sidestep all of the inconveniences because you knew you were on a dream-come-true journey that you had waited for all your life. Why don't more people transmute this same experience that I just described to fulfill their life by sidestepping life's challenges to live their dream life? The reason is that the largest percentage of our population doesn't stay inspired long enough. Most people find that inspired motivation is a struggle to maintain over a long period of time. When your life lacks purpose, you fill your days with diversions: TV, radio, movies, Harlequin novels, soap operas, drugs, alcohol, food, sugar, and the like.

What Do You Want?

Everyone has dreams for a better life: better relationships, more money, more quality time with loved ones, and better spiritual, emotional, and physical health. However, our dreams do not become a reality by merely aspiring for greater life benefits. Success and prosperity come from becoming truly inspired within. Your goals and vision become the driving force in your life, enabling you to go where you have only dreamed.

"Living Your Dreams" is a term we have all heard thousands of times. How do we actually create a reality from our dreams? Dreams that become your purpose are where the change of evolution begins. When your dreams become your purpose, success is your only option, much like the general who burns his ships off the coast of a small island when facing the enemy on the island. He sends a message to his men that victory is the only way off the island. The general leaves no way for escape. Most people in life have escape hatches and escape clauses in all of their dreams. When adversity and fear appear, the average person runs to their escape hatch to find their security blanket. This escape hatch is where it is safe and secure, warm and protected from all the danger that lies in front of prosperity's door and the door to freedom. I believe it is the fear of the unknown that paralyzes most of men and women's dreams!

Having a sense of personal meaning and purpose gives you a reason to get out of bed, motivated and inspired at the crack of dawn rather than sleeping in and putting off taking action on your dreams for fear you will fail—or for fear you might actually succeed. Having a purpose allows you to discover the whys of life. There may be many of them and they may change. I will caution you – your why better be bigger than just money. Shut off all the grumbling of other people who will give you all the reasons you will fail and tell you how crazy you are. Tap into your courage and come to grips with your fears and any unresolved issues of the past.

Your purpose will require you to sit in deep silence and listen to your quiet voice—the voice that knows who you really are. You are the only one who can decide what you deserve, what you can offer, and what will bring you your deepest sense of fulfillment and satisfaction. What is your calling? I am asking, "What will you be when you grow up?" Albert Einstein once wrote, "The man who regards his own life and that of his fellow creatures as meaningless is not merely unfortunate but almost disqualified for life!"

The meaning you give to your life—your purpose—is completely up to you. As children, most of us allowed our purpose to be defined by our environment and our family members in order to fit in and to meet the expectations of others. As an adult, finding your own meaning in life is far more individual and personal than that. I am talking about the fire inside that burns and propels you to higher levels of consciousness and personal and professional growth. All of us derive great pleasure in creating meaning and putting our own personal stamp on it. Why not choose a meaning that motivates and drives you, rather than letting the circumstances of life do the driving? Why not be more fully alive while you are here? Why not at least decide on a purpose to live life to its fullest and to enjoy every day and every minute?

Self-Fulfillment in Your Own Business

In your own business, you are the founder and CEO. It is time to develop and come up with a professional phrase designed to bring prosperity and abundance to you. Without a strong sense of purpose, you might quit when you are challenged. Committing to a professional purpose will prevent that from happening. Purpose fuels passion, and passion is what fuels prosperity.

Having a purpose and having a goal are two different issues. Purpose focuses on why you do something and has a much broader objective than typical goals. Goals are focused on what you do and are more specific in nature. Defining your why is so important to what you are doing. Why are you doing your enterprise? Most of you would give a knee-jerk reaction and say, "To make more money and be free, of course." These are good reasons, and they are the very same reasons I saw networking as a vehicle for me initially. Even at their best though, money, success, and fame are imitations of true contentment and peace of mind for creating a sense of belonging in the world. I am asking you to dig deeper here. Think about the options available to you just through your company and the actions you are presently taking.

With time and reflection, your why will become much clearer. Most people get so caught up in the day-to-day routines and struggles that their whole life passes without them ever identifying their whys. Time and money freedom is usually most people's reason or why; but what about change? Do you have a strong passion for the products and services you are marketing? Have you ever dreamed of being your own boss or owning your own business? Here is your chance now to take a step beyond the ordinary. What about leaving a legacy? Have you ever considered that you may be special, not just average? Is it a goal to home school your children? How about being in business with your wife, husband, or partner of your choosing? Does working from home rather than fighting rush hour traffic excite you? How about training and teaching and getting paid well for it? In our society, the average teachers are grossly underpaid. How about the opportunity you have to train people how to feel good about themselves and assist them in becoming successful? You can be paid very well for teaching this. Perhaps an industry such as network marketing can launch you to a successful career as a motivational trainer and speaker, like it did for me—does that excite you? How about the opportunity to develop strong bonds and ties with the people you train and teach? This industry also gives you the opportunity to hang out with other like-minded, progressive individuals who think out-of-the-box and ahead of the status quo. These are just a few examples of how to develop your sense of purpose to create prosperity and abundance in yourself and others. It's a win/win proposition.

Mary Kay Ash, the founder of the famous cosmetics company, Mary Kay, had a very strong purpose in her mind when she founded her company in 1963. Every representative who has worked with Mary Kay has been guided by the vision of this founder who was committed to encouraging women and especially recognized the worth that women contributed to the industry. She has been a tremendous role model and visionary for female entrepreneurs for more than thirty years and is responsible for developing many, many multiple six- and seven-figure income earners. Mary Kay started with a vision and a professional purpose, and she has definitely left a legacy. Her company was producing over $1 billion in retail sales in the mid-1990's.

Once you know what you want to personally get out of your business and what it is you desire to assist other people with, you will be set to create prosperity and abundance. It's not so much the money you want, but what money can buy. Knowing that you have huge amounts of money in the bank isn't peace of mind. It is knowing what that money can be used for that allows you to sleep at night. It's very important that you separate the idea of making money from the experiences that you desire to buy with money. As you grow, it is imperative to concentrate on enjoying and obtaining the experiences that will allow prosperity and abundance to flow much faster and more easily, instead of concentrating solely on making money.

There are a lot of negative connotations that many of us have associated with money, especially when money has been a struggle for many of us most of our lives. Contrary to popular view, money is not the root of all evil. The actual quote from the Bible states: "The *love* of money is the root of all evil." Just because it doesn't grow on trees doesn't mean you aren't entitled to your fair share of it. Negative thoughts about money will guarantee that you will drive it away from you. An easy way to bypass this problem is not to concentrate on money itself, but rather what you will do with it, because these thoughts are usually positive reinforcements for you.

Money and Prosperity Exercise

Think past money to items you would like to purchase and experiences you would like that bring joy, purpose, and meaning to your life. What do you want to use money for and how much will it take to satisfy you? Be realistic here; don't just say a billion dollars. The purpose is to find out what motivates you. Perhaps you would be motivated to dine in a five-star restaurant every night or to solve the hunger problem—or maybe neither. Do you want a home on a lake or in the mountains, a yacht or private plane? Put down on paper what situations you really desire to create in life. Remember, it can be a possession, situation, or experience that you desire to create. This will take some concentration. I challenge you to come up with at least 100 items on your list that you desire to experience or own in your lifetime. Once again, what really motivates you? Let it flow; explore your desires. Give yourself permission to really explore in order to find your purpose. Whatever you do, do this exercise without holding back; do it without limits to see how far you can expand. When you begin writing, you'll probably be uncomfortable at first, but keep going.

To prosper means to grow, to thrive, and to flourish. Abundance is an overflowing fullness or an overflowing quantity. When you have prosperity and abundance, you have plenty for you to flourish mentally, physically, spiritually, and financially. Money is really the representation of how much value you provide to the commercial marketplace. To achieve more money it is required that you become more valuable. You don't get paid for time in free enterprise, you get paid for how valuable you become in your time. Money comes to you when you provide something of value to a willing marketplace. Adding value to yourself through your personal growth is one way to create more results, as is catering to a larger portion of the marketplace. Most of the marketing in free enterprise is really about relationship marketing—through relationships you create through one-on-one contacts and referrals. This allows you a tremendous opportunity to create wealth.

Money alone won't buy you happiness; true fulfillment will not come from money alone. Happiness comes from within and seldom mixes with fear, desperation, lack, need, scarcity, and poverty consciousness. You are either in flow or in resistance. Prosperity and abundance only come in the flow state of consciousness. One of the easiest ways to experience a greater sense of prosperity is to take a look at where you are in life now and be thankful for what you have. Compare yourself to those less fortunate than you, and it will be pretty easy for you to feel some prosperity. Once you can detach from the fact that money itself is required to make you happy, then you can decide to acquire money and lots of it. You see, having money itself is not a problem, but how you feel about money and what you believe about money can be a huge problem.

Reaping and sowing is a term we often hear, especially in free enterprise and relationship marketing. Using the metaphor of planting and harvesting, we are taught to plant in the spring, nurture in the summer, reap the harvest in the fall, and then to prepare and store and sell in the winter. The metaphor of planting and harvesting is important to understand, because no sowing, no reaping, and no action all produce no results and no money. This is a rather predictable law of the universe. The downfall for most people is a direct lack of action, or not enough sowing.

Create clarity in your intentions. Ask the universe for exactly what you desire and be graphically specific. Don't make it a demand, don't plead or pray for it to happen, and don't bargain, saying things like, "If only you'll let this happen, I'll change—I promise." That's like saying, "Please give me water, and then I'll dig the well." Dig the well before you are thirsty. Make your request clear and strong. The best way to predict your future is to create it. You must change what you are to change what you will get.

Writing Ads to Yourself and the Universe

Use self-written ads to attract what you desire. For example, "Seeking seven motivated individuals to join my success team now. Must be hungry and willing to grow fast now! Must take action, teach others, become a leader, teach leadership skills, and be willing to make and share lots of prosperity and abundance. Like-minded only apply. Committed, not just interested, only!" Write out your own ads for what you will become and whom you will attract.

Remember, prosperity and abundance are created in the flow state of consciousness. Your actions and thoughts are directed in attaining and attracting, not in seeking money from a "I need money now to pay the bills" type of mentality. Moving ahead is not a solo job. There is no "I" in the word team. Include others in your thoughts. It keeps you more in flow. We are all connected, and each person you assist to prosperity creates more value in themself and most importantly in you. If you keep money flowing, you will always have more than enough, but if you attempt to horde or hang on to it, you decrease the supply and send a message of scarcity.

When circumstances challenge you, you must remain true to who you are and what you desire to become. Hold a vision of your life in your mind and stay focused, even if everything on the outside contradicts your dream. At times, you may be tempted to quit. You will build an emotional resilience just like a marathoner who hits the wall somewhere around the eighteenth mile of a twenty-six-mile run. Every nerve in your body may scream out in pain. Your mind may tell you to quit, asking, "What good is it if I'm not getting anywhere? I'm making no progress." No matter how much it hurts, marathoners concentrate on two things: the pain is only temporary, and the worst thing is to stop running. I have talked to marathoners personally, and they all say the same thing: "If you stop when you hit the wall, you will stay in pain. But if you keep running, holding the vision, you reach the point where you break through the wall and experience a rush of endorphins throughout your entire body, which eases the pain." The last few miles of a marathon are easier than the first few, because you begin experiencing what is called a runner's high. Hold the vision, focus your mental ability, attract your dreams, and take action over a long period of time.

As you grow personally and spend more time in flow, you will feel a change come over you. Many people will be shocked and some might be intimidated because you have changed. Someone once said that most people die at age twenty-five; they just don't get buried until they are seventy-five or eighty years old. You die inside when you fail to act and ignore your dreams. When you focus on your dreams, you will resonate with a strong, steady, positive energy. Money is just a flow of energy. Billions of dollars are flowing through the air, being transmitted through satellite communication every second of the day.

Begin to tune into the prosperity frequency, be thankful for who you are and what you are becoming, and realize that you are moving closer to true prosperity through your purpose and your why.

GETTING MONEY RIGHT
WHAT YOU DESERVE

Isn't it about time that you got right with money? When I say "right," what I am talking about is getting money right emotionally. Money is a very controversial subject in our society. Mention money to almost anyone, and it brings out a certain level of discomfort because almost everyone lacks money. Statistics say that 97 percent of our population works for 3 percent of society. Only around 4-5 percent achieve a six-figure income, and only one-twentieth of 1 percent of society achieve a seven-figure income. "Why is it," I ask, "that so many people struggle when we are living in a world with so many opportunities to create wealth?"

I have personally coached hundreds of great people in the last six years whose struggles with money issues have caused them to sabotage themselves over and over. One of the first questions I ask when it comes to money is, "Who was your role model when it comes to money, prosperity, finance, and abundance?" For most of us, it was our parents—and for most of them, it was their parents. Let's also state that this information is not about blaming anyone. You are now a grown-up, and your perception of money is now up to you.

The next question to ask is, "What did I learn in my education about money?" A typical high school curriculum includes courses about economics and government but nothing about how to attract money or how to have a healthy relationship with money. Traditional education teaches how to acquire job skills and prepares students to get paid what a particular job is worth, not what the individual is worth. Making more money requires becoming educated about free enterprise and how to get paid what the free market bears—getting paid on your terms and your time frame and learning about service and value. The more valuable you become through the service you provide, the more you make. This is not about working hard, because if that were the case, then all of the world laborers would be millionaires.

Over the centuries, money has gotten a bad rap by being associated with corruption, greed, pain, and the misuse of power. A perception grew that somehow the rich deprived the poor and that wealthy people were bad people, were not lovable, were disconnected from love, and were greedy. The sad fact is that most people just don't believe they deserve to have money freedom or peace of mind. I believe that you can be rich, spiritual, and prosperous, and that with your abundance you can create love and compassion, using your wealth to assist others to strengthen their skills so that they too have the opportunity to be prosperous in life's ways.

Remember, money itself is neutral, not good or bad. It is paper and metal that symbolizes an exchange of goods and services. Money is an energy that you either attract or repel. It is negative emotions around money such as greed, obsession, and power that can bring negative experiences and that keep most of us from it.

Getting Money Right Emotionally

Beliefs About Money Are Changing

Over the last several centuries, there has been a radical change in opportunity, philosophy, and ways to create wealth. Many courageous forerunners paved the way for new thoughts and ideas about prosperity, abundance, self-sufficiency, and enlightenment. Just in the last hundred years, brilliant writers and speakers have emerged like Napoleon Hill, Dale Carnegie, Earnest Holmes, Katherine Ponder, Florence Scovel Schinn, Earl Nightingale, Louise Hay, Jim Rohn and Tony Robbins, to name a few of my favorites that have assisted me with my enlightenment. A whole consciousness of self-help and personal development has become available to the masses. Bookstores and coffee bars are now as popular as some of the old traditional nightspots, and we now have access to coaches and mentors to be emotionally, financially, and spiritually fit.

Many people now realize that they are responsible for their own empowerment. They see that assuming responsibility can bring them prosperity and allow them to become more and do more. For this to happen, people require belief in themselves and grasp the idea that they can control their lives. In our me-too, microwave, lottery-mentality society, very few people ever put the proper thoughts and proper actions together at the same time to provoke the results they deserve. Plain and simple, most people don't believe they deserve prosperity and abundance. They want, they wish, they'd like to, if only, they pray for a miracle, and most of all they wait for change to happen. Sorry, it doesn't operate that way. Too many people tiptoe quietly to their graves, looking back only to say—"I wish I would have!"

Still, don't lose heart, for it can officially become "Now O'clock" at any minute. There are 86,400 seconds, 1,440 minutes, and 24 hours in every single day; one day, one week, one month, one year, one lifetime. We can change at any moment. Is it hard, or is it easy? You are one thought away from success or one thought away from failure. It is a choice we have the opportunity to make every single day.

The rules of money are simple. If you desire more money in free enterprise, create more value in yourself and your services. The more value you bring through the service you give, the more you make. In free enterprise, you have the opportunity to make what the free market bears. When you work a job, you get paid what the job is worth, and since the average jobs in America pay somewhere between $20,000 and $50,000, very few people ever get rich with that recipe. In today's rapidly changing market, you are required to think differently about how you will design your life rather than just make a living. Trading time for dollars is wages. Profits are where you can get paid what you are worth. We are all artistic, creative beings with brilliance inside waiting to get out and shine light on the dark. The world is waiting for someone like you to make a difference.

Take Leadership

There is a definite lack of leaders out there; are you one? Break free from "the thought police," get up, create some waves, rattle some cages, take risks, go to the edge, and most of all, not be consumed with what others think of you. If you are waiting for someone to give you permission to be successful, forget it. Success has a way of alienating and showing up people who tell you they love you. The only person who can give you success is you. Fame is something other people give you, while success is something you give yourself, and, just like beauty, "it is in the eye of the beholder."

I believe God wants us to be rich, prosperous, and free. God did not create fear; it is man-made. Fear overrides most people's dreams and objectives. Most people aren't even able to identify what they are afraid of. All they know is that they are struggling just to keep up with the other sheep in the pasture.

It is now estimated that 25 percent of America is involved in some measure in the self-help and the personal development movement. This is also referred to as "esoteric philosophy," or "new thought religion," and right in the mainstream of this consciousness is the truth that God is boundless wealth and that we have an opportunity everyday for abundant inheritance. The concept of abundance and self-reliance is being given a new image. Teachers have carried out the new idea, stating that it's now okay for individuals to take control of their lives, and that wealth, when used sensibly, is spiritual, desirable, and natural.

This is not to say that poverty is necessarily unnatural, for some people are born into challenging situations where they lack opportunity and education. We all have the opportunity to change, yet very few people embrace change. Most of society chooses to sabotage themselves and other in their circle of influence. We can all rise and change, especially when it comes to the right emotions about money. We can rise, no matter what the circumstances or how humble the origins. Average people let events shape their lives. This is a huge setback when it comes to producing the results they deserve. Past association with the pain of the past emotionally brought into the present is the thief of many a man's and woman's dream.

To change, we learn to change our perception of past events. We forgive and let go of old thoughts that don't serve us. We change our perception of old events. We believe in the invisible to borrow from the future. This is called vision: crystal-clear clarity on where you will be in two years and what you will become. The journey is the secret, for it is in the journey where you will find self-love. Self-love is the greatest gift you can give yourself. This can shorten the emotional distance between you and love, and between you and money. We are not conditioned to deserve either love or money, and we learn to enlighten ourselves with the right people, the right thoughts, books, tapes, and most of all, the right emotions—emotions that say, "I love myself! I deserve to have it all!"

Changes You Can Make

The difference between being poor and being a millionaire is not about one's talent, birthright, background, and upbringing. Talent has very little to do with generating and acquiring wealth. The world is filled with talented people who struggle their whole lives. An imperceptible shift in consciousness and vitality is required when it comes to attracting money. This shift can be simple and easy, or it can be difficult and hard. You can learn to be more open and place yourself in flow while learning the subtle law of money, abundance, and attraction so that life's opportunities come to you more naturally. It can be a part of your process internally and externally on your spiritual journey. I am not suggesting that all wealthy people are spiritual—some have simply adapted to the different marketplace of life. I personally believe that to be dynamic persons while living we learn to tie health, spirit, finance, and emotion together into one loving being.

I originally fell into "The Thought Money Trap." This was a trap that I laid for myself early in life by thinking that if I just made "x" number of dollars then I would be happy, content, and free. I had a series of magical numbers that I believed would fulfill me. They started out at $100,000 several years ago. I used to think, *If I just made $100,000 in one calendar year, then I could pay my bills, buy a new car, put a down payment on a house, have a two week vacation, and have a little left over to invest, and then I would be happy.* Then I perceived that $100,000 wouldn't be enough, and I continually raised the bar...$250,000...$500,000...$750,000...and finally one million dollars. I perceived that my self-image was tied to my status, my wealth, my possessions, and most of all, my consumption. I later realized that my money emotions were about consumption simply to make me feel better. Yet, in reality there was a tremendous distance between myself and love and myself and money. This distance was a very deep emotional distance that I had created over the years. It had slowly but surely become a veneer I had to put in front of myself to protect me from not only having money but from keeping it in motion. I later found there was a direct correlation between this distance, not only in money, but also in love.

Do What You Want to Do

I had spent most of my life doing what others had wanted me to do. I had played sports (which I loved) in high school. I enjoyed the competition, but I later realized I wasn't playing for me; I was playing for the recognition. I had never been loved the way I felt I deserved and had never been taught how to love myself, so for me, everything was based on the external: the flash, the sizzle, the look, and the consumption. I went to college, got jobs, and didn't fit in anywhere, wandering with a deep hole inside, looking for approval, acceptance, and most of all love, which I knew absolutely nothing about.

This confusion eventually created fourteen years of addictions, finally coming to a point where my destructive behavior had me at a rock-bottom, emotionless, near-death state. It actually took this bottom for me to stop the insanity, and through the grace of God I was able to get clean and sober for the first time in years. Life was better, but I still had to face the reasons behind my addictions. I delved into becoming successful and turned it into a passion. I read books, went to 12-step meetings, listened to tapes, attended seminars, took private counseling, and went to church. I explored hypnotherapy, acupuncture, acupressure, NLP, EST, retreats, sabbaticals, and many other resources, all with the intent of becoming a better person and becoming financially successful. I still believed that money would be the key my freedom. I later learned that what I really sought was peace of mind.

I started my own business and went through many ups and downs emotionally, spiritually, and financially. In my first few years, small changes began. I started to let go of my past, other people, and situations. I started to forgive and finally surrender. I surrendered my will to be right all the time. I was tested and I bent, but I never broke. I had to get a job twice, ended up $65,000 in credit card debt, and went almost two years without making any money. I was changing—my resolve strengthened, and so did my will to succeed, and my emotions got better. I started to learn about value and how to create it in myself for the first time. I learned how to keep my power instead of giving it away through my own anger and ego. I adopted a new philosophy that went, "You be right and I'll be rich." It was so refreshing to understand that the only approval required was my own. I learned no one would give me permission to be successful except me. I started to measure myself by my own standards, not someone else's. It's human nature to wonder, *How am I doing?* Everybody wants to know. The trick is to select your own set of standards, the ones that matter the most to you. This is where I believe we make it or break it.

You see, I had been measuring myself against an artificial set of standards: money and possessions—consumption. I believed that more was good. I started to achieve my objectives, and boy, I got good at the game! I was winning, making hundreds of thousands of dollars, but I was still unfulfilled. I fell into the very trap I had created. My addictions were based on consumption. When I realized all of this, I knew I had to change. I had to find what gave me pleasure and still allowed me to be my creative best. There was nothing wrong with the money and I enjoyed it, but it wasn't enough. I had to find my purpose. I realized that I had been in the game all these years not just for success and money, but really because I was searching for my calling, my purpose, and my mission in life. I was searching for a way to create more value and to give more service through what I was doing so I could enjoy more what I was creating.

I stepped out of a life of working for money and shifted to creating results for pleasure. I sold a business that was making me lots of money. I started over as a speaker, writer, and success coach, with no clients, customers, or products. It was a great challenge—I had no formal training and no idea how I would be successful, but I knew I would. I just knew it. Now I am doing absolutely what I love. It has become a passion, a love, a way to truly channel my creative passions on my time frame. For the first time in my life, I have become purpose-driven. I found a way to create value and service in a vocation that I truly love. I started to master the marketplace of life.

This will be a different challenge and a different process for everyone who seeks change. For me (and for most people), the greatest challenge was getting out of my own way—the feelings of lack, despair, and confusion. We get in our own way by placing thinking obstacles, detrimental ideas, and strange resentments in our path that we must let go of to get to our promised land. To get, we let go and learn what we already know: there is an abundant life, and we all deserve to be wealthy in all areas of our life—health, wealth, spirit, and emotions.

We also must realize that life is energy, money is energy, and there are plenty of both. Begin everyday by telling yourself that there is no shortage of money. It is vital to understand that it is not nearly as difficult as you perceive to become a millionaire; there are millions of people in the marketplace to whom you can sell your ideas, products, and energy so you can become a millionaire yourself.

Average Thinking Produces Average Results

We have been programmed by the system to believe that there are shortages and lack and that uncertainty is normal. It is not. Most people with a limited mindset have no comprehension of just how much money there is actually available to anyone with the will to "step up and collect." Because we are taught a fear of power, it is naturally assumed that somehow money is evil, that rich people are dishonest and crooked, and that they feed on the little people. While the economic forces of the planet are certainly stacked in favor of the big institutions and governments, there is nothing stopping each one of us from getting our fair share.

Get past the thoughts that money is bad and will somehow taint you. Money is neutral, not good or bad. Abundance is natural and spiritual. Money will not deprive you but could actually enlighten you. Many of the great teachers have given credence to the idea that abundance is spiritual and that it is your feeling and the power of your thoughts that create abundance for you.

If you are wealthy, more often than not you will be dispersing your money commercially and charitably, supporting many people around you and adding to the velocity of overall wealth. There are literally trillions of dollars passing through the world electronically on any given day, and those signals are literally passing by you at all times. If you stop and think about it, there are millions of dollars flowing through your body at the moment. Imagine making a slight flick of the wrist in order to stop some of that money in transit so it sticks with you. A flick of the mind is a flick of the wrist.

Money can be good—greed is not good. There are no reasons why you can't be very rich, very rich in fact, and still be a very valuable generous spiritual person with a huge heart and compassion for everyone.

Connect and Disconnect the Dots Exercise:

This exercise will assist you in identifying when your present money fears started and why they have been held in place all these years. The questions below will enable you to revisit the past and begin tracing long ago instilled subconscious memories and how they affect your life today. Focus on remembering your childhood and early adolescence so that you can review everything surrounding your thoughts about money. I would like you to focus on remembering everything you can about money, the good memories and the ones that may have brought you pain. Use the answers to help you fill in the ten worst things and ten best choices you have made with money.

1. What were the best presents you received as a child?
2. Did you feel you had nice toys? Were they as good as or better than your friends?
3. Did your mother work outside the home, or did she not work because you were well-to-do financially?

4. Did your grandparents give you money when you visited, or at Christmas or on your birthday?

5. Did you enjoy bringing friends to your house, or were you ashamed?

6. Did you have nice clothes, or were they hand me downs?

7. Did your family have a nice car, or were your friend's cars nicer than yours?

8. Were you embarrassed that you were better off than your friends, or were you okay with it?

9. Did your parents ever discuss money openly in front of you?

10. Did you ever see your parents fight over money?

11. Did you receive nice, thoughtful gifts, or did you receive money?

12. Was shopping for school clothes fun or drudgery?

13. Did you feel inadequate with the clothes your parents bought you?

14. Did you ever steal money from your parents?

15. Did you ever steal candy, toys, or anything else from the dime store?

16. Do you remember your first wallet or purse? Was it given to you empty, or did it have coins or money inside of it?

17. Did you collect coins or stamps?

18. Did you get an allowance as a child? If yes, was it less or more than your siblings or friends?

19. Did you spend your allowance, or were you taught to save a portion—or all of it?

20. Did you work at an early age?

21. What was the largest amount of money you ever saw as a child?

22. Did you receive money for your birthdays? If yes, were you told how to spend it?

23. Did you get visits from the tooth fairy?

24. Did you get paid for an "A" on your report card?

25. Did your family take vacations? If no, were you jealous when other kids got to go on vacations?

26. Did you ever go off to summer camp? If yes, were you glad you went?

27. What were your parent's perceptions about money—lack or plenty?

28. What did your parents tell you about money that made you feel good?

29. What did your parents tell you about money that made you feel bad?

30. Did you have a piggy bank as a child?
31. How old were you when you spent your piggy bank money?
32. Was your piggy bank full or almost empty?
33. What is the one statement you remember your parents always saying to you about money?
34. Did you miss out on playing team sports or other activities like tap dance lessons because there was a lack of money?
35. Did your parents buy you a car when you were sixteen? If no, how did you feel when other kids got a car and you didn't?
36. Did your parents buy your school clothes for you when you were a teenager, or did you buy your own?
37. Did you work after school or at summer jobs through junior high and high school?
38. If you worked then, were you able to spend the money, or did your parents require you to save it?
39. Did your parents pay for your college education or further schooling? If not, how did you feel when you had to pay your own way?
40. Did your parents pay for a sibling's college education, but not yours? Were you resentful if they did?
41. If you had siblings, did you all get equally nice or not as nice gifts from your parents?
42. Did anyone of your siblings receive nicer gifts than the rest of you? If yes, how did you feel about that?
43. Do your parents still help you out with money now that you're an adult?
44. If yes, are you expected pay them back?
45. If your parents are still living, how are they doing financially?
46. Do you loan your parents money?
47. If yes, do they pay you back?
48. Have you loaned money to anyone—family or friends—and not had it returned to you?
49. If yes, how did that make you feel?
50. As a child, were you told that money was evil?

GETTING MONEY RIGHT - WHAT YOU DESERVE

The 10 worst decisions I've made with or about money:

1.
2.
3.
4.
5.
6.
7.
8.
9.
10.

The 10 best choices I've made with or about money:

1.
2.
3.
4.
5.
6.
7.
8.
9.
10.

PART FOUR

THE SKILLS AND THE MINDSET

CONSISTENCY

Knowing what to do is not enough. A lot of people know what to do, but few follow through with a consistent plan of action that propels them to their dreams and goals. There is one trait that practically guarantees success in any field. Could it be talent, leadership, knowledge? Surely they can all contribute, but the single most important trait for guaranteed success is the ability to be consistent. From Henry Ford to Mother Teresa, the most successful people in any field are those who can stay motivated over a long period of time. A consistent plan worked over a period of time produces consistent results. Success is a marathon, not a sprint. In today's microwave society, the average person seeks instant gratification. If instant results are not attained, average individuals give up. They quit before their time. They throw in the towel, quitting "three feet from gold" as Napoleon Hill states in his classic book, *Think and Grow Rich.*

Most people never find their true calling, wandering through life, tiptoeing quietly so they can arrive at their grave safely, saying, "I wish I would have," or "If only I could have." These average people start projects, but seldom finish them. They rely on external events for their motivation, producing only spotty accomplishments that can never create the learning and persistency essential to success.

As a personal coach and mentor to thousands of people, I have found that the one key trait that separates success from failure is consistency. You either love what you do, or you create a way to love what you do. Get out of your old comfort zone. You will discover the discomfort is temporary, because it only lasts as long as is necessary for you to make the change you are looking for. Looking back, you will see that the vast majority of the discomfort was caused by your resistance to the change. Then you will get comfortable in an endeavor that will pay you what you are worth. In today's turbulent economy, you have probably already discovered that employees are paid what the job is worth to their employers. Thus with most jobs, you get only an illusion of security in exchange for a lid on your income.

Losers Play to Avoid Loss

We should play to win; however, most people play to avoid losing. This makes no sense. When you break it down, it's ridiculous. Motivation and consistency are the keys to success, but unfortunately, people have a hard time maintaining high levels of motivation and effort over a long period of time. This was the absolute key to my own personal success. My biography is the story of achieving a seven-figure income in twenty months. I was not an overnight success—it took eight years to get there. I paid the price over a long period of time with consistent action over and over with no results until I made personal breakthroughs. Even then I didn't collect the payoff right away. My secret was faith in the process and consistent action.

Let's take exercise for example. Most people know they should exercise, and some even start a routine. But how many continue that routine over a period of years to attain their desired results? It takes mental discipline and action to produce results. I trained as an athlete from the time I could walk. My father was a very successful athletic coach, and he instilled in me mental discipline, saying, "Son, you have to have more heart than the other fellows have talent"—a great quote I live by today. Heart beats talent every time. I'm sure you've heard, "It's not the size of the dog, but the bite in the dog that counts." This mental discipline that I learned at a young age has given me a tremendous edge on my own personal journey to my promised land of financial freedom and peace of mind.

I am a runner and a walker, and I am very consistent. I either run or walk three miles every day, seven days a week. I've missed one day in the last sixteen years. That one day was due to food poisoning, and I couldn't get off my bathroom floor due to my illness. There are many days

I don't feel like exercising, but I do it because it is my mental edge. My most creative thinking occurs during my alone time outside exercising. These are the times when I have the clearest visions. There are times when running is painful and difficult, but it is something I have done over and over again until it is a habit. Lack of consistency confounds most people's best efforts to achieve their dreams. Yet the technique for overcoming this problem is so simple and so effective that, if you use it, your life will never be the same.

Before describing the technique for maintaining high levels of motivation and effort, let me briefly tell you how I discovered a way to change the way you think and act. I noticed in my career as a personal coach and mentor that people usually know what they should do to improve their emotional, physical, and financial conditions. "Should" is the operative word. The problem is they don't "just do it." A basic rule of psychology is that people act to avoid immediate pain and/or to gain immediate pleasure.

Let's use credit card debt as an example. Many people have a history of going into debt using credit cards. They know that this is bad for their financial well being, but they still use them. Charging expenses helps them avoid immediate pain (that is, feeling they can't afford something) and adds to immediate pleasure (the joy of receiving a new purchase). However, the long-term pain of irresponsible credit card use is to be forever trapped in debt. Because that pain is not immediate, people continue to abuse credit cards.

I learned that for people to make consistent progress toward their goals, they require some form of immediate pain (or punishment) if they fail to take appropriate action. We all know we should do some form of exercise regularly and eat a healthy diet, but because there is no immediate punishment for failing to exercise, most people are not as consistent as they would like to be. But if every time you failed to exercise four times a week, someone came over and twisted your arm, you would be a lot more consistent. Now, none of you would hire someone to harm you if you didn't follow through on your goals. Therefore it works much better to find an immediate punishment you would be willing to give yourself if you fail to act in consistent ways.

Contract for Goal Getting

I call this my S.C.F.G.G., which is an acronym for "Success Contract for Goal Getting." Of all the psychological methods I've ever seen, I've never seen any technique have as much impact as this one. For this method to work, you don't have to like it, have faith in it, or believe in it. You just have to use it. Here is how it works:

Write a contract with yourself that states all the precise actions you are willing to commit to do during the following week. Then write a statement that says, "For each of the items on this contract that I fail to complete by one week from today, I agree to rip up two dollars." Sign the contract, date it, and put it where you'll see it every day. That's it —that is all you do. Here are some examples: "During the next seven days, I will exercise four days for at least one hour," or "I will read one book on motivation in its entirety," or "I will devote ten hours to prospecting in my enterprise," or "I will make at least one sale," or "I will organize my file cabinet so it is neat and orderly." "For each task I don't complete I will rip up two dollars."

Tearing up money can be a painful thing to do. This exercise will work with all people; it will work with unmotivated people, motivated people, lazy people, and even people who don't believe it will work for them. There are several reasons why this method is so effective. First, there is a stated purpose in what you plan to do and by what date you intend to do it. Most people have a lot of lofty thoughts about what they could do to improve or change their lives, but these often get put on the back burner. With S.C.F.G.G., you will have a visual reminder of what you are going to do. You will also experience immediate punishment if you fail to keep your word. Don't forget that your brain is always trying to avoid pain and suffering, and it will do its best to complete what's on the contract.

You are probably wondering about the significance of destroying two dollars. Having seen this technique in practice, I have found that two dollars usually works best. When people write down that they'll rip up a five-dollar bill or higher, they often fail to rip up the money. Instead, they make up excuses as to why they couldn't finish their contract, or they just blow the whole thing off rather than rip up that bill. On the other hand, some people find the threat of ripping up two dollars enough to get the job done, but if they don't complete their contract, they're willing to rip up the money to avoid going back on their word.

It's OK not to complete everything on your contract as long as you rip up the money for any uncompleted tasks. As long as you are willing to rip up money for failing to complete your contract, the method eventually works. Maybe not the first or second week, but by the third week people usually master it. They find their mind screaming at themselves to complete their tasks. After a period of time, the S.C.F.G.G. method will become your most trusted ally.

RAISE YOUR DESERVE QUOTIENT

The concept of deserving is of great interest to me. Deserving surely appears to be the area of life where hidden and often unaddressed thinking patterns from people's unconscious minds have the greatest effect. I know many people who diligently perform the same tasks that make others successful: making calls, attending meetings, reading uplifting books, and listening to personal development audio programs. Yet their positive results are either miniscule or nonexistent compared to others who perform the same or fewer activities. This inconsistency means it is essential to look beyond the obvious—beyond the events that take place—to account for the difference in results.

I use the terms "deserve quotient" or "deserve psychology" to describe the invisible factors that unintentionally determine people's results. The reality is that all of us deserve to have it all. Yet so many people believe that having it all is impossible for them. These people end up sabotaging themselves. Every day of the week, intelligent, motivated people unintentionally sabotage their best efforts by using strategies they are completely unaware of. As one of my clients stated to me once, "I always figure out a way to snatch defeat from the jaws of victory. I am my own worst enemy."

Over and over again, we see in the media, in our friends, and in ourselves how this sabotage operates. For many people, sabotage is the most frustrating part of life. The voice we often hear is "I just can't do this," "This is too hard," or "I don't deserve success." Sabotages are self-imposed chains and shackles on our behaviors and feelings, restraining us from getting what we deserve, even though we desperately and determinedly want it. This thought process is so contradictory—why in the world would we do this to ourselves?

I have discovered that fear is the operative agent in sabotage. Whatever we fear, if we fear it long enough, it will happen. If we fear abandonment, we will abandon first—and often we abandon ourselves as well as someone else. In other cases, fear of abandonment causes us to unconsciously behave in exactly the way that will drive others away. If we fear rejection, we reject ourselves first. If we fear success, we make sure we don't get it. Our unconscious mind thinks failure is bad enough, but success might be worse. If you fear intimacy, you'll pick people you can never get close to. Whatever you fear, if you do not confront and resolve it, the fear will win and you will lose.

As Gerald Jampolsky says in his book *Love Is Letting Go of Fear,* "The world we see that seems so insane may be the result of a belief system that isn't working. The belief system holds that the fearful past will extend into a fearful future, making the past and future one. It is our memory of fear and pain that makes us feel so vulnerable. It is this feeling of vulnerability that makes us want to control and predict the future at all costs."

Fear creates results by causing the mind to focus on the occurrence of the unfavorable event that is feared. By focusing on what we fear, we attract it to our reality. By trying to control our lives so it won't happen, we give energy to its occurrence as a sabotage to our dreams. We have all heard that "fear is the thief of our dreams." Fear is a four-letter word that creates paralyses and keeps so many people stuck in their present circumstances.

The challenge for all of us is to face our fear, to be in charge of it, rather than letting fear be in charge of us. Until we face fear, it will win every time. Fear doesn't stop just you—it stops almost everybody! The essential challenge is changing fear into faith. One- percent doubt does not equal 100 percent faith. Unless we change or face it, we can be assured fear will win every time; fear will guide our behavior and our decisions in ways both obvious and subtle. This is our sabotage. The first step in mastering fear and raising our level of consciousness is to be in charge of

RAISE YOUR DESERVE QUOTIENT

our fear rather than pretend to have no say about what we deserve.

Sabotage plays a huge role in keeping people from believing that they truly do "deserve to have it all." Here are just a few of the most common sabotage patterns. Each is followed by a description of how they limit our belief systems and hold us in place.

Resignation

Deep down I don't believe I deserve it, so I won't even go after it. I don't like to get my hopes up, because then if I don't achieve my objective, it won't hurt so much.

Throwing It Away

I get it, and then because I don't believe I'm good enough, I throw it away. This sabotage is very common in professional sports, especially with athletes from terrible home lives.

Settling

I think I want it, but I'm not sure I'm good enough, so I'll settle for less. I won't try very hard, because I probably won't get it anyway.

Denial

I won't pay any attention to this problem. Hopefully it will just go away.

The Fatal Flaw

People who use this strategy may advance themselves by taking all the right steps, but they have a crucial personality problem—perfectionism, excessive drinking, being a hothead or an overreactor, having a hot temper, or overwhelming guilt that undoes all their best efforts. This sabotage is very common, and it's the one I identify with the most.

Blaming

This is probably the most common of all the sabotages. Everyone, everything, and every excuse are used to place blame except on the right person. This is a way to intellectualize all the reasons not to take

101

responsibility for both actions and lack of actions.

Poor, Poor, Pitiful Me

This sabotage is very common with people who are ill or injured all the time. These people have a chronic problem usually related to getting attention.

Poverty Consciousness

This stems from programming of grandparents and parents. It is the by-product of lack and scarcity, always thinking that money is tight; there is never enough; you will probably lose it if you have it. Rich people are bad; rich people cheat; rich people think they are better than we are. Poverty consciousness involves the mentality of "holding on to whatever we have or we will lose it."

What each of these sabotages has in common is an underlying sense of not deserving the desired goal. The key to changing your subconscious sabotages is to become explicitly aware of your own internal deserve quotient. Once you understand that which has been outside your conscious awareness, then and only then do you have a chance to change it.

Your Deserve Quotient is comprised of your conscious and unconscious beliefs about what you can and should achieve in your life. Your deserve quotient is a gauge or degree to which you believe you deserve what you seek in various areas of life. These deserve levels are self-chosen and can be changed. Of course you consciously believe you deserve to be happy, financially stable, prosperous, secure, loved, and free of guilt and negativity. Many people read books, listen to tapes, and tell themselves daily they are changing, and they believe it consciously.

You were probably taught the so-called Golden Rules—if you worked hard, were a good student, obeyed orders, and used your head, you would get everything you desired out of life. This is the unconscious reward system, where you earn respect with good behavior. The other side of this distorted view is that when bad things happen, it was probably your fault.

You should have thought about what you did before you did it, and so you deserved the bad result you got.

The concept of earning or controlling all of the outcomes of our life is impossibly flawed. You cannot control major acts of God, the economy, or other people's feelings. The good news is that you are in charge of your own choices, feelings, and behaviors. This is where you can make a change. Before you can have more in life, you must first understand that the maxim "Know thyself" refers not only to your conscious awareness, but also to your unconscious mind.

This means changing at a deep and profound level. Some changes come quickly and easily, while other changes take longer and may not be so easy. You must have both a commitment to and faith in the evolutionary process of change. Success is the process of going through changes to collect the payoff. The rewards at stake are huge. You can have more in life than you ever dreamed possible.

It is completely up to you to decide how and what specifically that "more" is for you. Perhaps to you, achieving more means more income, more to donate, more loving relationships, more peace of mind, more self-empowerment, more spirituality, more health, more wealth, and more energy.

Most people already know about the stress and pain of deeply wanting someone or something, yet feeling chronically blocked from getting it. There is frustration in trying. The painful irony is that *trying* doesn't work. You may know someone right now who is desperately trying to quit drinking or smoking, lose weight, or give up some other unhealthy habit. Releasing fear is your goal—not just in any particular endeavor, but in every aspect of life. Many people have lived in fear in one form or another throughout their entire life. They have never given themselves the opportunity to play the game. They prefer not to take the risk of losing, because it might be too painful. They don't consider that they might also win. Winning and success is an attitude. It is a state of consciousness that says, "I will not be denied."

The only way not to feel the anguish of fear and frustration is to fully understand the how and the why of sabotaging behaviors. Your final decision about what you believe is influenced by all your beliefs and feelings, both conscious and unconscious. There are specific desire levels for every area of your life: love, work, friends, and health. Paradoxically, it is possible to have a high desire level in one area and a low one in another.

You were born with the fundamental right to believe the best of yourself. This entitlement is basic to everyone and every human being. Somewhere along the way, most of us begin to doubt ourselves and our desires. As children, there was no question about our right to be loved and held. Infants ask for what they want without hesitation, and when they don't get it, they respond spontaneously and fearlessly.

Something happens as we grow older—our innate sense of deserving to feel our feelings and express our desires gets lost as we become socialized. Instead of believing we deserve love just for existing, we lower our self-esteem to earn approval and love by performing and conforming. We begin to think we must earn love (usually by seeking approval), so we give up our authentic desires to conform to the expected standard image. At two years old, most children are fearless. But as we get older, we begin to limit our beliefs and abilities. We conclude that the other guy or girl can make the team, score the points, become the cheerleader, get the job or big sales presentation, get the advanced degree, and get the girl or guy, but not us! These feelings and beliefs sabotage our confidence. They drain our psyche and our physical energy. Subconsciously, many people are defeated before they begin. There is no longer a competitive spirit in them (in their perception)—they say, "I'll give it a try," but in their hearts, they are defeated before they begin. There is no will in the word "try." Try is a weak word.

Change Is a Process

Change takes time; it is an evolution. It can be a short time or a long time. Deserving more means that you will expand your beliefs, your feelings, and your spirituality. This is where you must learn the laws of the universe and take action both internally and externally. This is an inner journey, a unification that becomes an outer reality. There are no accidents. Deserving more means a purposeful alignment of your beliefs, action, choices, focus, and energy.

With my clients, as in my own life, I have come to understand that we don't allow ourselves to have what we want until we believe that we deserve it. I have found that we truly get what we think we deserve. This is exactly why many of my clients have a difficult time believing they truly can be free, prosperous, and happy. They have never been given permission to think and feel this way, and they have never given themselves permission either. Our psychological comfort zones limit our deserve level. When we achieve beyond our comfort zone, we face a choice: either our deserve level limits expand to encompass the increase, or we let it slip through our fingers because deep in our subconscious, we still don't believe we deserve to have the results we have achieved.

Our beliefs about what we deserve subtly create our reality. Some people live out this reality through constraints rather than flourishing with the vision of the possible. To have a full and happy life, seek a balance between what you want and what you believe you deserve. This balance is determined by your personal expectations. The negative expectation says, "I don't deserve it, so I'll sabotage getting it." The positive expectation says, "I deserve it, so I'll facilitate getting it."

You might remember in the movie *The Empire Strikes Back* when Yoda said, "Believe in the Force, Luke." Luke said, "I don't believe it." "That is why you will fail," Yoda replied.

The process of growing up could be thought of as an eighteen-year course called Life Beliefs. This course covers all areas of your life: where

PSYCHOLOGICALLY UNEMPLOYABLE

to go to college, what courses to take, your career path, religion, style, success, whom to marry, and which pleasures and friends are acceptable. This is a complete course by age eighteen. It's taught to us with daily lessons and homework assigned by experienced teachers, usually our parents and grandparents. The material they teach us has a lived-in reality about it, because it was also taught to them as children.

We take on these beliefs from the people we grew up with. They are not always the beliefs they expressed verbally, but rather the ones they acted upon and lived out. Many times in our sessions, my clients say, "It's scary. Sometimes I sound just like my mother or father." I know—I have said it myself. They are surprised to realize they are responding in a similar way to their parent's responses.

Beliefs are repetitive statements you make to yourself, often about yourself. In most cases, you accept them as absolute truth. Like all of us, you grew up in a family that instructed you by word and deed about what life was to be for you. You were schooled in beliefs and expectations for yourself, created by others. Whether you knew it or not, you signed an emotional contract that stated what you were entitled to, but you probably missed the small print. This covered your thoughts, decisions, feelings, and values. As you grew up, the power of this emotional conditioning continued to assert itself, and your beliefs are reflected in the people you choose to love and be close to, the career you choose to establish, the amount of money you earn, and your level of physical and emotional health. Thus, your deserve quotient was formed unintentionally at an early age and continues to operate without your awareness.

The reality is that all of us deserve to have it all. The only thing that stops us is inside of us. In particular, these obstacles are our beliefs, our programming, our self-esteem, and our lack of self-confidence. At this point in your life, it is now time to change! Change is what will bring you the results you deserve. This is a process of reinventing yourself. This is a process of change that you have the opportunity to experience. Be committed to letting go, facing your fears and turning them into faith, and understanding that in order to have it all, you must give it all. Give yourself permission to be successful. No one else will give you this permission. Give yourself this gift of approval. This is an abundant universe. You can have whatever you desire, and it all starts with you understanding that you deserve to receive everything you desire!

ATTRACTING QUALITY PEOPLE

You attract to your reality who and what you are. Entrepreneurs typically have tremendous products to market, and they have a vision of establishing a tremendous company to create true financial freedom. Most entrepreneurs are working diligently to develop themselves. Attracting quality people to your life and your enterprise is an essential key to success that receives little attention.

Life is really a life of networking. We develop relationships, form friendships, raise families, develop business contacts, and, in an even broader sense, we are all connected in one way or another. As an entrepreneur, it is very important that you understand the dynamics of what is required to be successful and how you can apply this information to your personal life.

Perhaps you have heard the cliché: "Your net worth is directly proportionate to your network." You are in the business of developing a professional network, and your team starts with you being the leader that other people are looking for. There is no "I" in the word team. You can't and won't make it alone. Teamwork and duplication are essential. Attracting quality people to your enterprise and choosing the right people is paramount to the success of any enterprise. The best way to make this happen is for you to become the right person. Choosing and attracting the right people to grace your business and your life is a skill that can bring a life of total fulfillment. You require other people to appreciate your special qualities and service. You can be the greatest person in the world, but if you don't have others in your life who recognize your talents and appreciate your specialness and unique qualities, then life has very little meaning. A lot of qualities will come into play as you start to develop yourself into a terrific person. Just to name a few: your charm, character, class, charisma, (I call these the four C's), leadership ability, intuition, integrity, desire level, work ethics, and ability to care for your fellow teammates. We not only require people to acknowledge us and share our intimate feelings, but we require people to make our lives successful.

You will fail if you ignore the most essential element necessary for reaching your goals: attracting other people who can assist you and whom you can assist in reaching their dreams and goals. Entrepreneurship is really a business of developing yourself and the people around you. Some of your greatest rewards will come from watching other people grow and prosper. Of course, it is wonderful to be wealthy, brilliant, rich, and famous, but if you have no one to offer a kind or encouraging word to or share things with, all the wealth and intelligence in the world become meaningless.

No matter what you do, you require other people to make your life worthwhile. If you want to live a fulfilled life, you will learn that you do not get to the top by yourself. The most essential element for entrepreneurs is learning how to find, attract, and keep the people that will bring joy in your life. Take a good look at the lives of successful people, and you will quickly realize that they have all had terrific people in their corner, offering guidance and support. When they didn't have direct support, they found a way to model themselves after other successful people. The role models I have selected for myself are exceptional entrepreneurs such as Jim Rohn, Tony Robbins, my father, my grandfather, and one of the most brilliant idea creators I have ever met, Mark Victor Hansen.

Many of you are probably asking, "This sounds great, but where are all the great people?" I have asked that question myself. There were times I talked to hundreds of people, and none of them had the qualities I was looking for. The key to all of this is to attract great people. The first step is for you to become what you are looking for. You do this by learning from others, from the books you read, from the tapes you listen to, finding role models, being mentored, and taking action. When you learn to heal yourself you can also heal others.

Like many of you, I have had my moments where I felt shy, insecure, and uncomfortable in social situations. Like you, I have felt the pain of being rejected and the frustration of not being able to move forward because fear and shaky self-esteem paralyzed me. Like some of you, I have felt lonely, empty, and scared through fourteen years of drug and alcohol abuse. I didn't have a drinking problem; I had a living problem—a problem of self-esteem.

Today I no longer feel that way, because I have found and continue to find quality people who are happy to work with me rather than against me. What a great concept! I no longer feel as though I am on the outside looking in. I have also learned how to become a quality person myself and give back what the quality people in my life gave to me. As a result, I have never been happier or more fulfilled. As I have attracted terrific people into my life that have assisted me in living my dreams, my confidence level has grown, my career has blossomed, and my social life has flourished.

A frequent question I hear from clients and those attending my seminars, and from business associates and friends is, "Where are all the good people?" I hear single women say, "Are there any decent men out there?" I hear men say, "All the good women are taken." I hear things like, "Most prospects are losers," or "I can't trust anyone," or "It's a dog-eat-dog world," or "You can't trust anyone." These are self-defeating perspectives that many people unintentionally adopt. Many have lived through horrific challenges: bad marriages, abuse, addiction, and abandonment (both emotional and physical). They live out these experiences over and over by attracting bad situations and bad people to their reality. Then these people enter an entrepreneurial endeavor and continue this pattern by attracting bad clients and partners without understanding why. We attract who we are. What we think about, we bring about.

There are actually millions of terrific people in the world. If you haven't found any yet, become one now!

Do something exceptional; become exceptional and you'll attract exceptional people!

Terrific people are right in front of us every day, but most of us don't even recognize them. Look around you; you are in a business where interaction, leadership, personal development, and commitment are required. You are not a man or a woman on an island. We not only require people to survive, but we require them to succeed.

People with self-esteem issues usually suffer from thinking they are not such terrific persons. They unintentionally push terrific people out of their lives because they feel they don't deserve them. A terrific person is someone who allows others to realize their own self-worth. They bring out the best in everyone they meet.

Feelings of unworthiness are exemplified by "The Groucho Marx Syndrome." Groucho joked, "I wouldn't want to be a member of any club that wanted me as a member!" Only after you acknowledge your fears, confront your inner demons of unworthiness, and eliminate all the wrong information that has been programmed by the toxic people who previously infected your life can you feel that you deserve the best that people have to offer.

Having self-esteem, confidence, abundance, and peace of mind is what we all seek. I have received letters and cards from people all over the United States that have moved me to tears thanking me for making a difference in their lives. These are terrific people, and this has allowed me to reflect on my own life. These are the best possible gifts I could receive—enriching the lives of others so they can go on to enrich the lives of others.

The central theme of this chapter is finding abundance, freedom, and peace of mind through developing yourself and developing others at the same time. To attract quality people into your life and enterprise, you must visualize the quality people you seek. The way to do this is to truly envision whom you want to work with, who you'd like to have as friends, what you're looking for in a spouse, and the kind of teammates you seek. List the qualities you desire on paper. That's right; create a profile of exactly who you are looking for. List at least thirty-one qualities. This produces a list long enough to challenge you to make it complete. Give yourself a descriptive and clear visualization of exactly what you are looking for. To visualize these terrific people in your life, close your eyes and look inward. Visualize the types of people you want around you. Are they as committed as you? Make sure what you are looking for is quality big thinkers—and people who really care about themselves and others. Don't prejudge based on your first impression.

Where Do I Find Terrific People?

This type of attracting is referred to as "in-visioning." Practice this daily—speak it into existence. It has worked wonders in my client's lives—and in my own life. It will do the same for you. Bringing quality people to mind can bring them to you in body!

Here is a list of twenty-five places or activities to give you some ideas of where to begin!

- Taking a brisk walk
- During your daily routine
- Doing errands
- Walking your dog
- Waiting for a bus, plane, train, or other transportation
- Working out at a gym
- Waiting in line at a movie theater
- Participating in a sport
- Attending a sporting event
- At the office: yours, theirs, and other people's
- At a business meeting
- At a doctor's appointment

- At a health spa
- At a coffee shop or restaurant
- In a house of worship
- At any party or social event
- At a reunion
- While shopping
- At a seminar or lecture
- Getting your car, video, computer, or any appliance repaired
- At a music or video store
- At a library or museum
- At a political activity or function
- In an elevator
- At any special event: christening, birthday party, wedding, anniversary, graduation, etc.

You may come up with ideas of your own. Be creative and don't be afraid to explore new ideas. Remember that it is up to you to make the first move and initiate contact. To get, you must ask. The answer to the question of "Where do I find terrific people?" is that you find them everywhere. A quality you will start to develop is bringing out the best in others. Concentrate on making others feel good because they matter to you through your caring and kind words. Attracting great people will always start with you. I'm sure you have heard the saying, "Before you can love another person, you have to love yourself." Perhaps the great playwright Oscar Wilde summed it up best in the following quote: "To love oneself is the beginning of a lifelong romance." The starting point is in how you treat other people. The better you treat others, the better you become.

Virtually every major religion holds to that philosophy and shares a universal truth —"what you give, you will receive." Reciprocity is the key to being a quality person.

Whether it is as the Old Testament says: "Casting your bread upon the waters and having it return to you," or as the New Testament says: "Reaping what you sow," or the Hindu philosophy of "Enkarma"—doing good for others and having it return to you—or the Buddhist philosophy of "Cause and Effect," or even the old Japanese adage—"When you do for others, the gods will repay you," there is surely a reciprocal relationship between giving and getting. When you learn to give for the sake of giving, then through this act you end up receiving. There is a Chinese saying that sums it up best: "When we give someone a rose, the scent of the rose also lingers on our hand." Being a terrific person means you are giving, generous, helpful, and caring; you are a leader, sensitive, kind, and empowering others consistently.

Keys to Attracting Quality People to Your Reality

- Your self-esteem—how you view yourself—a positive self-image attracts positive people. A negative self-image attracts negative people!
- The first ten seconds—you never get a second chance to make a first impression.
- A smile and a warm hello—smile and the world smiles with you; snore and you sleep alone.
- Attracting terrific people by the way you speak—it's not what you say, it's how you say it! Develop confidence in your voice.
- Your body language—60 percent of all communication is nonverbal; 40 percent is verbal. The way you carry yourself—carry yourself with confidence. Send a message that you are a terrific person and a leader.
- Improve your communication skills! Find your areas of weakness and make a commitment to improve (and…um…mumbling…you know…like)
- Identify your future clients, partners, mates, and situations—put the

qualities you seek on paper and focus on them.

- Affirmations—speak into existence and magnetize these people to you.
- Become a terrific person yourself. Focus on that aspect. You deserve to have it all. You attract to your reality exactly who you are.

MASTER THE ART OF LISTENING

Listening is different from hearing. Hearing involves your ears only. Listening will directly impact your potential for retail sales and finding new clients or partners for your business. Your ability to listen effectively will have an influence on your capability to develop relationships, effective questioning and information gathering, as well as your potential for developing rapport and gaining your audience's attention.

There are three distinct levels of listening, and it is probable that you will discover that you have never learned how to listen effectively. The good news is that you can become a great listener starting today!

Level one is where most people spend their listening time. This is pretending to pay attention. In other words, you may listen to the first half of what someone says, but you are really focused on what you will be saying next. You may even begin to talk and literally forget that you are supposed to be listening.

Level two is when people really do try to listen. However, they don't truly put much effort into it, and they certainly don't actively participate in learning more about the speaker by listening intently. It's an unemotional, very logical listening method that attempts to make sense of the words.

At the third and most effective level of listening, people give the speaker their full, undivided attention. They really are listening! This is called active listening, and it means listening not just for the words, but for the meaning behind the words. By developing your listening skills to the third level, you will see immense improvement in your sales and entrepreneurial efforts.

Active listening begins with you giving encouraging body signals and expressions and by asking questions. You can and should control the listening process. Only one third of the speaker's meaning is actually conveyed by words. Two thirds is conveyed by body language, indicating emotional tone. Pay particular attention to your body language and that of the speaker.

Toward Better Listening

Becoming a good listener requires practice, patience, and a genuine interest in other people. Here are several suggestions you may use in order to improve your listening skills:

1. Make the speaker feel comfortable and important. Be courteous and respectful.
2. Show your attentiveness to the speaker by nodding your head or saying "Uh-huh" or "I see" from time to time.
3. Listen to what is *not* said. Pay attention to the 80 percent of the conversation that is nonverbal. Learn to listen between the lines. By doing this, you will be in a position to really hear beyond what is being said to what is meant.
4. Listening between the lines will assist you in detecting when your potential customer is being evasive or dishonest with you. You deserve to know the truth, even at the risk of seeming a little pushy. By honing your listening skills, you will be able to catch anything in your speaker's voice, attitude, or body language that would indicate a lack of real interest or enthusiasm for what you are offering.

I have found that many of my clients fail at retailing or developing new clients because they are unwilling to listen for the truth when they hear it. In many cases, they simply hope that what they are hearing is different from what it sounds like. In other words, the potential client is saying through their body language or tone of voice that they have no interest in the opportunity or products being offered. Often, my clients miss this "not interested" message completely because they either didn't want to hear it or really didn't hear it because they were too focused on what they were going to say next.

Filters

Understanding listening filters can improve your effectiveness greatly. As people listen, they filter what they hear through their own mind and experiences. If you are not careful, this can significantly distort what you hear. As a result, what you hear may not be what the speaker said or meant.

For instance, suppose you believe that only women can be organized. So if the speaker says, "He was very organized and efficient," you may hear, "She was very organized." This is because you weren't listening carefully, and in your mind the second statement is the closest to one that makes any sense to you.

I will outline some of the listening filters you should be aware of. In each situation, any one of these filters can distort what you or the other person hears and understands.

- Beliefs
- Values
- Interests
- Assumptions
- Attitudes
- Viewpoints
- Memories
- Strong Feelings
- Prejudices
- Expectations
- Past Experiences

Now that you are aware of and able to recognize listening filters that may cause you to not listen fully, let's talk a moment about the barriers that can reduce your listening effectiveness. Improve your listening right now by removing any of these barriers:

- External distractions, such as noise, movements, or the speaker's mannerisms may be a diversion to you.
- Daydreaming (your mind wanders)
- Physical exhaustion (inability to pay attention)
- Internal distractions (preoccupation, stress)
- Being self-conscious
- Interrupting
- Paying attention to only the things that interest you
- Lack of trust or respect for the speaker
- Not listening to nonverbal language of speaker
- Taking too many notes, so that you miss much of the speaker's information because you are focused on your note-taking

Reflective and paraphrase listening are two techniques which will assist you to reinforce to your audience so that you are, in fact, listening to them and are aware of their concerns and point of view. Reflective listening is merely repeating some words your partners or customers use as they speak. For instance, your client may say, "I was involved in free enterprise before, and I received no support from my mentor." You respond, "No mentor support, huh?" and leave it at that. Allow your client to continue speaking. Reflective listening builds rapport in three ways: It shows that you are paying attention and that you understand what your client is telling you; it is a great strategy to keep your client talking long enough for you to evaluate whether they are serious or merely curious; and it's a great way to keep developing rapport while you wait to get down to the real issues.

I don't recommend that you spend a long time listening to each partner's or potential customer's complaints about past products, companies, or services. Paying attention and listening is a good investment of a few minutes of your time in the preliminary interviewing stages. It is better to listen and find out right away they are not interested than to find this out after you have invested a lot of time in a lengthy presentation.

Paraphrase listening works on a similar principal, except that you paraphrase what your client has just said. For example, if your client says, "I've spent a lot of money over the years in other ventures." You would say, "Yes, becoming a successful entrepreneur has a price."

Be sure to use both active and reflective listening to enhance rapport and keep yourself on your toes. It will assist you to keep your client talking until you are ready to make a decision about whether they are serious or merely curious about your opportunity and products.

I teach my clients how to interview people to see if they are the type of person they would like to work with. Many people confuse "interview" with "interrogate." By practicing the shared listening technique, you will find that all of your questions get answered without the other person feeling as though you have them under a microscope. Shared listening allows you to turn the questioning process into a conversation. Here's how it works:

I might ask my client, "So, Bob, what do you do for a living now?" and he may say that he is a teacher. I would then say, "No kidding? Both my parents are teachers. How long have you been a teacher, Bob?" Bob responds by saying, "Twenty years—where do your folks live?" I would say, "They live in Iowa. Wow! You've been a teacher for twenty years…. Why are you considering an entrepreneurial endeavor, Bob?"

The Art of Conversation

Developing a conversation, rather than asking one question right after another, is a great way to get a person to open up. Other people are more comfortable revealing information about themselves if they feel you have something in common. It also makes them understand that you are a real person and not a robot simply asking questions. Listen closely and make brief notes for yourself. By interviewing in this fashion, you will soon discover their motivation or lack thereof, as well as their hot buttons, which you can repeat back to them when it's time to ask for the decision or close the sale.

It's not only important to listen at the beginning of your interview. It is equally important to continue the listening process even after you have closed your sale with your new partner or client. Much of my success as an entrepreneur, trainer, and now personal coach has been achieved because of my willingness to listen. It astounds people that I'm able to recall names, places, and other pertinent information with little or no effort. I'm able to recall this information because when it was being given out initially, I paid attention! Once again, I listened!

Listening is the key when it comes to remembering people's names. Another way to show sincere interest is to remember a new acquaintance's name after you've been introduced and use it later in the conversation.

Remembering Names

Here are a few tips that can assist you to better remember names:

- Repeat the name immediately after you hear it
- Use the name immediately after hearing it
- Write the name down as soon as possible to etch it into your subconscious
- Associate the name with something or someone familiar to you

I've heard it said that people love to hear one word spoken out loud more so than any other word. Can you guess what that word might be? If you said, "their name," you are correct. Don't underestimate the power in remembering and then speaking a person's name.

Men and Women Hear Different Things

Do men and women have different listening styles? Scientists believe that we learn our listening behaviors one step at a time. Newborns and infants up to eighteen months old have shown no noticeable sex-related differences when it comes to listening. However, by two years old, researchers document differences associated with sex. The sex-related socialization we experience as children and the stereotypes we use as adults influence how we listen.

Men and women sometimes experience challenges in communicating with each other due to different sex-based listening styles. Believe me, there are exceptions to every rule, so don't be surprised if your style of listening doesn't fit perfectly in the "male" or "female" examples. I will list for you a few sex-based stereotypes:

Men	Women
Logical	Emotional
Dominating	Caring
Defensive	Responsive
Judgmental	Empathetic
Impatient	Attentive
Arrogant	Patient
Inattentive	Understanding

Numerous studies have assessed the effectiveness of men and women speakers and presenters. The consistent results suggest that listeners remember information better when they listen to male speakers.

Women tend to recall precise words and phrases after a conversation. Unless the situation calls for it, men retain only general ideas. Men seem to hear the facts during conversations and lectures without paying much attention to other details.

For instance, a man will give a vague outline of a conversation he had with someone. When pressed for specifics, he might say, "We didn't really have much to say to each other; we talked about the weather, the conference coming up next week, our children, and the inflated gas prices. That was about it."

If you asked a woman about the conversation she had with someone, you would more than likely get this type of explanation: "Mary and I stood and talked for twenty minutes. We were both enjoying the weather, and she mentioned how nice it will be for all of us if the weather continues to be nice since we have that conference coming up next week on Friday. She and Bob are going to drive their new Mercedes instead of flying. Even with the gas prices being so high, driving is still more reasonable for them than flying. They'll be bringing their children along with them; remember, they have two boys and one girl."

Notice the difference in who spoke in specific terms and who was likely to generalize? Again, this example is stereotypical; however, it does illustrate that there are times when it would seem men and women do come from different points of view when listening and communicating. In order to avoid stereotypical labels, both men and women can improve their ineffective listening behaviors.

Generally, Men Should:
- Work on understanding and interpreting feelings in conversations
- Avoid interrupting others
- Listen instead of attempting to provide immediate solutions when a woman is upset or complaining
- Check for rigid or overly assertive body language, such as crossed arms or holding eye contact to the point of making the woman feel uncomfortable

Generally, Women Should:
- Be more assertive when having a conversation with a man
- Be patient when men tend to interrupt too much, and develop an assertive, not aggressive strategy to create space to finish a thought without interruption
- Avoid reading too much emotional meaning into men's verbal and nonverbal messages
- Keep voice tones level and even, rather than high pitched and loud

- Display confidence when discussing business issues

Listening can strengthen family and business relationships. Marriages and business partnerships are created, maintained, and/or destroyed through effective communication. Most important is our requirement to really listen without assumptions when discussing emotional topics, such as marriage, child rearing, money, and responsibilities.

If you learn to listen before speaking, before sticking your neck out, before taking an unreasonable position or making commitments you are unable to keep, you will likely avoid many unfortunate experiences.

Listening carefully will greatly reduce much of the stress associated with being an entrepreneur. By tuning into your partner or client with your undivided attention, you won't have the tendency to become emotionally attached to someone who is merely looking and not buying.

In my 8-CD audio series, *The Psychology of Prospecting*, I talk about listening to the words people speak. By listening and tuning into other people's language, you will be better able to learn about the person on the phone or sitting in front of you. Are they using use words of empowerment or the exact opposite? Are you listening for words that would indicate a self-starter or potential leader? Can you hear sincerity and enthusiasm in their voice, or is the person you're speaking with dull and unmotivated?

How about you? Do you listen to the words coming out of your own mouth? Are you in tune with your voice inflections and tones? Do you sound defensive when someone asks about the quality of your products and services?

Listening to others is crucial, but listening and being aware of your own communication skills is where success begins. I often recommend that my clients use a cassette recorder to tape themselves when they are conducting a product presentation or an interview.

Sometimes what you thought you said or meant to say is not what comes through the recorder when you play it back.

Developing good listening skills requires a proactive, ongoing approach. With practice, you too can master the art of listening!

The
Psychology of
PROSPECTING & CLO$ING
Special Offer

Learn the skills Jeff has developed and perfected to create multiple seven figure income results so that you can become a Master Prospector and Master Closer now!

This Information Will Assist You To:
- Attract prosperity partners
- Turn your prospecting time into money
- Interview prospects from your peace
- Master the art of listening
- 3-way calling techniques that produce results
- Get your point across in 30 seconds or less!
- Master the art of asking
- Effectively trial close
- Operate with a constant "sense of urgency"
- Identify and close the four main personality types
- Release your fear and stay in your power
- Neutralize the 5 most common objections

Retail Value = $293.00
Order Today for ONLY
$149.00 + S&H!

Visit Our Special Offers Online!
www.GoldenMastermind.com

Releasing Rejection

I have learned some valuable lessons in my entrepreneurial endeavors. I have discovered that the opposite of rejection is not just acceptance; it is also perseverance. In my many years as an entrepreneur, I have definitely learned to persevere.

When someone else's words or actions produce misunderstandings and hurt feelings, it is because you are taking it personally. These actions and words are interpreted as rejection, and your emotions take over. Your knee-jerk response is all out of proportion to the event itself and is most likely a reaction to rejection experiences dating back to your childhood. Now new hurts and the stinging reality of "Nos" pile on top of old hurts, and it is as if each cutting remark and "No" opens up old wounds that are never healed.

As an entrepreneur, it is very important that you get a clear, true handle on rejection. This chapter will assist you with how to handle rejection and not take it personally.

Your Emotional Filing Cabinet

Over the years, signs and signals, tones and inflections, words and phrases all pile up emotionally. These childhood rejection wounds may come from parents, teachers, siblings, aunts, uncles, grandparents, baby-sitters, or neighbors. Whether these wounds were intended or not, they often become self-rejecting beliefs that can tinge your adult relationships. Anything in that group of people or situations can trigger a defensive response that is larger than life. The very reason that most people are fearful of picking up the telephone to find new clients or new business is they "fear rejection"; they fear hearing the word "No." They take it personally, they hold on to it, and they feel like they are a failure or did something wrong. This fear of rejection is what paralyzes people from reaching their dreams. I call this phone phobia or phone fear.

When people experience a frightening incident like a physical attack, or an upsetting episode like a verbal attack, they may not only be reacting to the shock of the present crisis, but may also be reacting to all of the previous traumas they have experienced dating back to their childhood. Enduring rejection is similar. You may not only be reacting to the present situation but to past experiences as well. Some of these experiences may have been traumatic, and as a child experiencing them, you may have felt betrayed, violated, or rejected, making it difficult to trust that world is a safe place. These feelings of rejection can stem from a lack of parental love or the inability of a parent to express the emotions of love—this is a major cause of why people fear rejection. I have assisted many clients with overcoming these same issues.

The Past Was Different

Consider the era when your grandparents and parents were raised. It wasn't as common back then to express emotions the way it is today. There is a whole different awareness of expression today. Did you ever hear the saying, "Grown men don't cry?" Grown men in their thirties, forties, and fifties often didn't know how to express their love for their children, wives, and families. It was "implied" in their words, and their loved ones were supposed to figure out the fact that they loved them without them verbalizing it.

The fear of rejection is a situation that haunts a large percentage of our population, and it also stems from abandonment issues, both physical and emotional. It is very prevalent today in single parent homes where one parent has left because of a divorce, a death, or some other reason. The child grows into adolescence, then adulthood, and then becomes an entrepreneur and has no clue why they can't pick up the telephone to find new business or talk to people in their circle of influence about their enterprise.

Fear is what rejection is really about – fear of the word "No." Have you ever talked to someone about your business, and they ask you if cold calling is involved? You can already sense their fear. I have had many people say to me that they could never pick up the phone and call people, because they do not know how to market their products or services. They perceive that they will receive too much rejection; they perceive that people will say "No" to them before they ever get started making calls, and they perceive that this process will be painful.

Entrepreneurship is really about collecting decisions when you break it down to what I call the ridiculous. This means breaking each situation down so far that you begin to realize how much your emotions from your past are making each situation seem much larger and more challenging than it actually is. As an entrepreneur, you are in the business of exposing people to your products, services, system, leaders, your confidence, and your opportunity. It works like this—no exposure, no results. I can't tell you how many people I have seen get started with a new business or a new endeavor who are extremely excited; they get all their ducks in a row, get set up, get trained, even quit their jobs in some cases to get prepared for this new enterprise. Then the day comes when they receive the opportunity to make the calls that will begin to fulfill their own dream, and they are paralyzed by fear. They perpetuate this by "getting ready to get ready," which is really just procrastination. They shuffle papers around on their desk all day until they are exhausted enough to pass out, and then they fool themselves into thinking they put in a full day at the office. As an entrepreneur, you do not get paid for time. That is what a job does—trade time for dollars. As an entrepreneur, you get paid for results, and you have the opportunity to get paid what the free market bears for your energy; this is called free enterprise.

High Achievers

This is why entertainers, actors, authors, athletes, and entrepreneurs achieve what ordinary people call "outrageous incomes." They get paid what the free market bears. Do you realize that only 3 percent of Americans achieve a six-figure income? Only one-twentieth of one percent achieves a seven-figure income. The alarming situation is that so many more could achieve these levels of success, yet most people are paralyzed by fear, and fear of rejection is the number one fear that keeps people stuck!

To release the fear of rejection, we must first understand this challenge so we can live in the solution. Fear of rejection stems from two main fears: the fear of being abandoned, and the fear of losing our identity. These fears stem from our earliest years when we learned about relationships from our parents or other caregivers. Because we were so dependent on them for care, we felt vulnerable to their whims. We required their comfort and love to establish our identity and self-esteem. At times, we worried that they would leave us, and sometimes one of them did, and we came to fear the rejection of abandonment. At other times, we became afraid that our parents would overwhelm us with closeness, smothering our own identities. Other times, their love was conditional, based upon our performances. "Don't even come home with bad grades," or "How did you drop the ball?" or "How could you lose the game?" This type of emotional abandonment can go on for years, and often we do not truly understand it until we are well into adulthood. Perhaps many of you can identify with what I am saying. This was not our parents' fault; they were this way because they were also products of the way they were raised—it was generational. This type of emotional abandonment was the very core of my fourteen-year addiction to alcohol and drugs. Forgiveness is where I began to heal.

Other times we have over-protective parents or extremely strict parents that rob us of our identities—another rejection. How does this happen? They may not let us show any independence or creativity or assertiveness or a sense of our own individual identities. These rejection fears created by abandonment and intrusions accompany us through life, causing no end of trouble in our personal lives, our relationships, and in the opportunities of business.

Fear of Rejection Goes Beyond Business

Fear of rejection has led many of us to hesitate about asking that special person out on a date to a movie and dinner, and it has held us back from asking for a raise on a job, submitting our artwork or manuscripts, writing our first novel, and even asking for a favor or a ride to the airport. We end up intellectualizing all these reasons not to do something out of fear. I have had many people not call me for assistance out of fear, convinced that I would probably be too busy to assist them. Amazing! I get messages saying, "Mr. Combs, I am sure you are probably too busy to work with me." I have clients who hire me and are afraid to tell me about their lack of action from the previous weeks. Guess what held them back the previous weeks? They have made no calls and taken no action out of fear of rejection, which is the same fear that keeps them for asking for assistance by being honest about where they are struggling. This fear stifles our creativity and blurs our dreams.

Your Foundation of Rejection Is Ancient History

It assists us to understand how adult rejection issues are rooted in childhood. Most of us wanted to be loved, cared about, and respected, but perhaps that didn't happen when we were growing up. What if you wanted to be comforted by your mother, but she held back? What if you wanted your father to listen to your stories about the school play, but he just kept reading the paper, not paying attention to you? Did you ever want your parents to attend your athletic games or school plays, and they did not show up? Do you remember how great it would have felt to be praised once in a while instead of having been chastised for the time you made mistakes? Wouldn't it have been nice once in a while to be told you did a good job, even for a small situation like doing your chores? I have a client who once achieved mostly "B plus" grades, as well as a few "A minuses," and his father wanted to know why all his grades were not "A minuses." My client said at this point he gave up and quit trying to achieve good grades, realizing that he could never please his father.

How many of you have been laughed at or teased because of your heritage or the color of your skin? Perhaps you were taunted because you had to wear hand-me-downs or came from "the wrong side of the tracks." How many of you were picked last for teams in grade school games and were humiliated by the other kids? How many of you flunked a test or failed a grade, or perhaps dropped out of school or just plain did not fit in? Many people perpetuate these same tapes over and over their whole lives, holding on to past traumas of rejection. I hear it in people's voices every day, and I can feel their pain. I know, because I have been one of you before. These old tapes of the past are coded deep into our subconscious, which is the memory bank that stores all of the messages we receive during our lifetime. Our conscious mind has no memory, yet our subconscious mind stores everything.

Years later, we are still affected by these childhood wounds. The old wounds take their toll, and we are stunned when these old tapes get triggered and reverberate into our adult lives and relationships, causing even little challenges and situations to set us off. Our feelings are easily hurt by the words, actions, and behaviors of others. This is what keeps us from picking up the telephone to make the necessary calls required to take action in moving closer to our dreams. It keeps people stuck making a living and just getting by instead of designing a life and becoming the person they deserve to be.

Taking situations and events personally can get in the way of your business and personal relationships. Sensitivity to rejection can be a symptom or an attribute of a number of psychological issues such as adult attention deficit disorder, depression, self-esteem issues, stage fright, eating disorders, highly sensitive nervous systems, shame-based issues, shyness, and other types of abuses and addictions. Rejection, however, is more than another slice of pie—it is the crust that overlays all the issues.

Really Not About You

What is the answer to overcoming these fears that limit you and keep you from living your dreams? The very first key is understanding that it is time to stop taking life personally. If you don't make sales, if you collect a lot of "Nos" on the journey, you realize it is all part of the process. The lesson is in the process. It is not what you receive, but what you become on the journey that counts. As Harvey Mackay writes in *Sharkproof*, "Don't rationalize away the hurt... Point your head in the right direction and get back in the game."

A "No" is not a permanent condition; nor is your present status in life. Start to view everything that used to hold you back as short-term. Realize that there are no failures; all roadblocks can be turned into building blocks if you change your philosophy. Start to view every situation as part of your education on this journey to freedom. Adopting a philosophy of "It is not what I lost, but what I gained because of this situation" will allow you to achieve the results and success you desire and deserve.

Tools for Releasing Rejection

Stop Overreacting

Begin creating room between the events in your life and your responses to these events, so that you have time to evaluate what is happening and formulate your *response* rather than to simply *react*. Most people simply react to the situations they face before they have taken time to evaluate what is really happening. The truth of the situation is that when we are reactive, we often actually overreact initially and then realize after the fact that our reaction was completely out of proportion to the situation. I also refer to this as majoring in minor things. As you continue your growth, begin to give yourself time to breathe and respond to the challenges that you face.

Create a More Thorough Analysis of the Situation

Is your response to the situation at hand appropriate? Take moment to analyze all aspects of what is really happening. Often when we take our emotions out of the equation, the solution effortlessly appears.

Change How You View the Situation

Learn to look at all sides of an issue and understand that you are interacting with people who carry the same emotional pain as you. Begin treating and understanding other people as you would like them to treat and understand you. When you realize that a situation is not personal, it will allow you to understand the reasons why people behave the way they do, and when you have mastered this skill, you will begin to neutralize potentially explosive situations before they get out of hand.

Understand the 80/20 Principle

This simply means that 80 percent of the results you receive will come from 20 percent of your clients. Focus your time and energy on the people who are growing and changing so that you can partner with them to produce more results together than you could individually.

Seek Mentors Who Have Overcome Your Same Situation

Spend time with people who have experienced the same challenges that you have and overcame them so you can learn how they handle adversity. Seek role models and mentors that have already been through the process of change so that you can model your behavior after theirs. Teach yourself to learn by example instead of "learning everything the hard way." This simple step can greatly shorten your growth curve and allow you to create the changes you seek much more quickly.

Become an Objective Student of Your Challenges

This also relates to the principle of nothing personal in business. Learn to appreciate your strengths as well as recognize your weaknesses from the same emotional perspective. Learn to be an observer of yourself and evaluate your strengths and weaknesses objectively. Become your own biggest fan and begin praising yourself for your progress so you can overcome your challenges instead of continuing as your own worst critic.

Live in the Solution

Most people spend tremendous amounts of time focusing on their problems. I suggest that you learn to live in the solution. Ask yourself how you can grow, what you can learn, and whom you might meet because of your experiences rather than dwelling on the problem, which does not serve you.

Borrow from the Future

Learn to let go of the past and stay focused on where you are headed. Borrow from your faith in the future rather than continuing your attachment to the past.

Read Books on Self-Esteem and Self-Confidence

Become your own best teacher on how to improve. Find books that will serve you to build a better self-esteem, such as *Don't Take It Personally: The Art of Dealing with Rejection* by Elayne Savage, Ph.D.

Understand What a "NO" Really Is

A "No" is not about you. A "No" is really about the person giving you an objection buying into their own validations and excuses. The people who choose to say "No" are the same people who rarely allow themselves to say "Yes" to opportunities or to life. Remember that opportunities are never lost; they are always taken by the people who are ready.

Live in Faith, not Fear

One percent doubt does not equal 100 percent faith. Begin to live in the faith that you are growing and changing and improving; believe that you deserve to live your life on your terms. You deserve to achieve your dreams now!

Forgiveness Exercises

Write letters to people from your past who you feel have wronged you. Forgive them for their actions or inactions, forgive the situation, and then forgive yourself for the role you played. Then burn the letter and let it go. This is a powerful exercise and a great way to begin creating peace.

Mirror Exercises

Spend two minutes each night in front of your mirror saying a series of affirmations to yourself while you maintain eye contact with your reflection. Create your own affirmations, such as "I love myself; I deserve to have it all. I am lovable. I am good enough. I am changing. I am growing. I am creating new life circumstances that are empowering to me and my family now." These are a few examples of affirmations you might say. Your beliefs are created by a series of statements you perceive to be true. This is the power of practicing positive affirmations daily.

Sort Out the Facts Before Diving Below the Fear Line

Is there really a present situation to fear? Are you creating reasons to not take action that do not exist? Take the time to look objectively at the facts before seeking shelter behind the fear line. You will often find that you are creating an emotional mountain out of a molehill of reality.

Get Past the "What's Wrong With Me" Syndrome

This goes back to focusing on the solution rather the problem. Stop being a victim of your own drama and realize that each and every one of us faces challenges emotionally born from the same pain, the same abandonment issues. We all express them differently, but we all carry the same burdens. Start focusing on "What Is Right with Me," and I guarantee you will experience quantum leaps in your growth.

Assume Responsibility for Your Happiness

Only you can choose to be happy or unhappy. Find reasons every day to give thanks and feel gratitude for your situations and circumstances. I have seen millionaires who are as unhappy as struggling entrepreneurs. Decide that you are responsible for your own happiness. Make this decision now and then take action to create the result. No one but you will ever give you permission to feel happy and satisfied.

Evaluate Your Childhood Experiences

Evaluate how your childhood experiences were not your fault. Your responsibility now as an adult is to understand that you were not to blame and that you can take action to change your perceptions. You learned a value system from your parents and caregivers as a child. It is now your responsibility to determine if these values serve you and to release those that do not.

Change What You Are Passing On to Others

Take a look at your actions and what you are teaching others. If you are passing your limiting conditioning on to others, begin to make changes that will empower you and others.

Practice Saying "I Have a Choice"

The lesson here is "I have a choice about how I react, how I respond, the language I use, and the situations I create."

Learn the Art of Detachment

Begin to neutralize people by agreeing with them. "You are absolutely correct" and "Thank you, I am receiving" are two of my favorites. Take your emotions out of the equation and allow the other person to have some room to be right. When you can detach emotionally from the outcome of a situation, you will create space for a win/win situation.

Take Action and Learn from It

T.T.P.—Talk To People and see what happens. Learn from your conversations and go T.T.M.P.—Talk To More People!

Make Your Actions Consistent

When your actions are consistent every day over a period of time, you will begin to experience consistent results. Condition yourself to engage in the daily activities that move you toward the goals you seek.

Change How You Have Been Changing!

Is change easy, or is it hard? Is success a struggle, or is it a privilege? If you are sick and tired of being sick and tired, then I suggest you consider changing the way you have been changing. Allow change to become easy—go with the flow, release control, and experience life.

Place Your Order to the Universe!

Make a decision about where you are headed and what you are doing. Create your statement, mail in your order, and lick the stamp. If you have been waiting for permission to succeed, give yourself this permission and state your intention with the expectation that because you are taking the proper actions, you will receive the results you desire in a time frame that you deserve.

PART FIVE

HABITS AND FOCUS
BREAKING IT DOWN

WHAT IS SUCCESS?

Success is an attitude. Success is a habit. Success is attainable to all who desire it, who believe they deserve to have it, and who are willing to turn their desires into action.

Success has no secrets. When questioned, those who have been successful are quick to tell about their complete devotion to attaining their goals and dreams. They speak of the commitment to developing their craft with passion and zest. The theme is always the same: "They paid the price for the privilege of their success."

Creators of great fortunes or even some level of financial stability tell us that money served as part of the dream, but only as a by-product. When you listen to such people, they describe how they followed their passion. They attribute their success not to fate, but to the conscious and methodical application of very specific principles. Many would say that perhaps luck played a very minor role; however, that is true only when "opportunity meets preparation."

I'm a firm believer that success is a process and not a pay off. The key ingredient necessary to become successful is DESIRE. Money, age, race, education, and physical appearance matter very little—much less than most people think. Desire coupled with a willingness to change is the real prerequisite to success. Just how badly do you really desire to achieve your dreams?

Successful people don't sit around waiting for success to come to them. They design their own fate by taking matters into their own hands. Your life and ultimately your success are your own personal responsibility. How great is your desire to create the life you imagine?

Average People Operate from a Position of Fear

- Fear of failure
- Fear of success
- Fear of rejection
- Fear of commitment

Fear truly is the thief of your dreams!

What Precisely Do You Want to Accomplish?

When making a decision to become successful, it is important to be very clear about your dream. What is your dream? Unfortunately, average people tend to have very average dreams. In personal coaching sessions with my clients, I often ask the question, "What is your dream?" The sad fact is that many of my clients will tell me that their dream is to get out of debt. So in other words, getting back to zero is their lifelong purpose? I don't think so.

It's time to move past your day-to-day concerns over your bills. Yes, these are real, but if you make your bills the focus of your thinking and motivation, then by the creative power of your mind, you will simply create more bills. We all have bills and financial obligations. However, I challenge you to think beyond your debt and to begin visualizing yourself achieving an objective that really moves you. Remember that when you are pursuing a goal with passion and an unrestrained focus, the money will be forthcoming if that is what you truly desire.

Do you have a vision of your success? Can you feel your success? Does it have colors and a location? Perhaps your success is being involved with a cause or a nonprofit organization designed to assist and empower your fellow man. Give life to your dream by making it even more detailed than it is now. Can you see it? Feel it? Hear it? Smell it? Taste it? Successful people create a vision or a blueprint of their mission. Do you have a vision of your ultimate achievement? Is your vision so strong and moving that you could literally reach out into the thin air and lay a hand on it? In the following chapters, I will assist you in creating your vision for your future and for your success. I will walk you through a step-by-step process for your vision creation.

Success Myths—What Success Is and Isn't

Success will be different for every individual who desires it. First and foremost, success is not about money, fame, fortune, wealth, or toys. Success, in reality, is an experience, a process, and a challenge. It is an opportunity for you to become more and to achieve more. Success will be a different experience and a different process for every one of us. It is indeed unique to each individual.

Like many people, I went through my own personal challenges, including fourteen years of alcohol and drug addiction. Following this, I experienced a series of close successes followed by let downs, failures, pink slips, terminations, bounced company checks, changed pay plans, and companies going out of business (just as I was about to make a quantum leap). I eventually ended up $65,000 in credit card debt, discouraged, but determined to stay the course.

I experienced a lot of what looked like failures on the outside, yet on my inside they were really more reasons to overcome, to grow, to learn, and to begin to change myself. There are no failures. Instead, I viewed these experiences as essential feedback. Every blade of grass I've walked on has led me to this present moment consciousness!

What happened? How did I finally become successful? How can you too become successful in life? We all deserve success, but how do we actually achieve it? Isn't that the seven-million-dollar question? Here's what happened for me, and it can happen for you too. I changed! I didn't change overnight either; it was an eight-year process for me. Most of you are going to go through some changes of your own.

I hit bits and pieces of success along the way, but it took eight years before I had any monumental success.

How It All Started for Me

It all began with change. I changed my thoughts. I changed the people I paid attention to. I changed my mind about how I viewed failure and success. I changed my opinions about my parents and myself. I changed what I read, what I watched on TV, and whom I associated with. I changed some very deep-rooted decisions I'd made as a small child about who I was as a person and who I would become. I changed my views on many things, including the government and corporate America. I changed the way I thought about how to become free in all aspects of my life through free enterprise. Self-employment was my ticket to success.

It wasn't easy to change, but I did it—and so can you. I struggled at times, and more than likely, you will too. I made a conscious decision to be different and to do different things than I had done before. Then I kept making those new decisions over and over again, with no emotional attachment. Eventually these new ideas caught on in my mind, and I began to apply my new knowledge. I got hungry to achieve, and I took action over and over again regardless of the outcome.

Almost everyone I have ever met desires health, wealth, and peace of mind, yet so few are able to achieve all three. Why is that? How many people do you know who have achieved one or two out of the three? Sadly, most never do.

Most people think that if they work harder and for a longer period of time, they will eventually have success. To become wealthy and successful, you'll soon discover that hard work isn't the answer. You don't get paid for time when you're self-employed, as I am. You get paid for how valuable you become. Trading time and working hard for dollars usually gets you broke.

Look at our national statistics. The purchasing power of American wages from jobs is now more than 20 percent below what it was in the mid-1970s. This means that pay raises have fallen way short of keeping pace with increases in the cost of living. Across the board, double-digit pay raises are a thing of the past. More recently, there have been more than a million job cuts since the 9/11 terrorist atrocity. The recommended income producing plan that you learned from your parents—get a good job with a stable company and work your way up—has become a blueprint for failure in the New Millennium.

Success means personal growth, action, and change. It is detaching from people, things, and situations. You must be willing to detach from the people who love you, but who tell you that you will never make it! When I say detaching, I mean mentally and emotionally detaching. Success is moving forward constantly toward what you desire. It is being in the process—it's change coupled with action, and it's being in love with the process. Success is getting everything you deserve and feeling great about yourself!

The true secrets to success are found in the process, in self-motivation, and in the internal emotional fire that leads you to act powerfully. Notice I said "self-motivation." What is self-motivation? It is belief, confidence, courage, posture, self-image, and creativity. It is the internal drive that allows you to take action continually despite the circumstances.

To achieve your goals, you must become self-motivated. Reading books, listening to tapes, and saying affirmations are all great places to start and to sustain motivation. Remember, without action, no results are created.

Thirteen Qualities of Successful People

1. Successful people have dreams.
2. Successful people are achievers.
3. Successful people have drive and determination.
4. Successful people are focused.
5. Successful people learn to take action.
6. Successful people take responsibility for their actions.
7. Successful people look for solutions to their problems.
8. Successful people make decisions and stick to them.
9. Successful people can admit when they make a mistake.
10. Successful people are self-reliant.
11. Successful people live in the process of constant improvement.
12. Successful people develop leaders.
13. Successful people have enthusiasm for the process.

There are many doors, many paths, and many trails to becoming successful. Success, like beauty, will always be "in the eye of the beholder." People who excel in life are those who produce results—not excuses—for themselves and others.

The bottom line is that success is found in doing and accomplishing, not in owning and possessing!

TIME
YOUR MOST VALUABLE COMMODITY

Regardless of your company, product, or services, what you are really selling is your time. What we are really selling is our time in free enterprise. Most people don't have a true concept of money; they don't realize that time is money, and almost everyone gives their time away.

ROI, or Return On Investment, is a common term in corporate America and in investing. What is much more important to the entrepreneur is "ROTAE" is Return On Time, Action, and Energy. These are your strongest resources. You can't afford to waste time. For most people, time works against them as an enemy. Successful people use time as an ally. There are 86,400 seconds, 1,440 minutes, and 24 hours in a day. Success is not really about what you do, but what you do daily. Time is your most precious resource, and everything you produce is a by-product of how you manage yourself in your time.

On a daily basis, I devote fourteen to sixteen hours to my craft, my personal development, and my self-empowerment, which I truly love. I don't for a minute consider that devoting this much time is work. When you love what you do, it is pleasure, not pain. When I sit down to do my tasks, I know what I desire to accomplish, and I make good use of my time.

As I stated earlier, most people don't have a clear concept of either time or money. Mention money, and people become very uncomfortable. Mention time management, and you get similar responses. When it comes to time, the average person equates time with work, and they perceive that they have to work hard. In free enterprise, we don't get paid for time, but trading time for dollars is what most Americans do over and over. This activity is called a job, and jobs usually keep people broke, because they are paid what the job is worth. The average person brings the mentality of a ten or fifteen dollar per hour job to free enterprise, including the predominant belief that if they work real hard they will get rich. Occasionally this philosophy works, but not very often.

To be successful as an entrepreneur, your thoughts about time and time management must change. The free market pays you for results, not time. This means that if you desire more income, your value must increase in proportion to what you desire. How valuable you become through services you perform is the key issue. The question you should be asking yourself is, "How do I turn time into money?" Your effectiveness in managing your time is going to have a direct impact on your overall long-term results.

In my numerous years in this industry, I've found that there are four phases in the way people manage or mismanage their time:

1. Spare Time
2. Part Time
3. Full Time
4. All The Time

Unfortunately, most people confuse themselves and think they are doing one of these last three phases, when really they are spare time.

The Paradox of Time Management

Time management is really a misnomer, because time itself is really unmanageable. Time is a resource that is constantly being depleted at a predictable rate—60 minutes an hour, 24 hours a day, and 365 days a year. What we do have the ability to do is to manage ourselves in a way that will make effective use of time. This is an important distinction that can assist you to take the stress out of your life and put more productivity, satisfaction, and freedom into it. Efficiency is distinctly different from effectiveness. Efficiency is completing a task. Effectiveness is completing the task and achieving the desired outcome. Effectiveness is measured in results, and when you are an entrepreneur, results are everything.

Almost all of us would like to make better use of our time. A common mistake we make is to try to do what we're currently doing more efficiently. It is a good idea but the wrong starting point. It doesn't matter how efficiently you manage your time if you aren't spending it pursuing the results you desire. Your most effective use of time is the action part of the process. Eighty percent of your time should be spent marketing, not shuffling papers, reading books, listening to tapes, gossiping, procrastinating, getting ready to get ready, and the multitude of other excuses you can use to divert your attention from the very physical activity that will pay you. Do the right tasks inefficiently, and your business will survive. Do the wrong tasks efficiently and you go broke. Take the right action efficiently, and someday you'll be set for life. Efficiency is only valuable when it contributes to effectiveness.

Becoming successful requires a mindset that creates urgency— urgency in numbers, in actions, in tasks, in leadership, in all areas. Successful people get tasks done now. This is self-motivation. Average people don't take on this sense of urgency; they get around to things when they feel like it, and this is usually too late, because they procrastinate. The ability to distinguish between urgency and importance is crucial to creating and living successfully. The inability to distinguish between the two gets many people in trouble and ultimately results in broken dreams and shattered lives.

Every day we have situations that arise and situations we are required to address. Some are urgent and some are important, some are both, and some are neither. Doing what's urgent first is big mistake, because it too often leaves what is important undone. Begin today to understand: urgent situations are seldom important, and important situations seldom appear to be urgent. Most people spend 80 percent of their lives responding to the urgent as if everything urgent was important. You must learn to separate the two. Do this by taking the proper action with a sense of urgency, but not with a panic or fear-stricken mindset. For instance, closing a sale, or enrolling a client to use your product is urgent, but developing a flourishing organization is more important. Having a new car and wardrobe is urgent for a lot of people. Saving, investing, and developing a prosperity conscious is much more important to become financially independent.

If you spend your time overreacting to the tyranny of the urgent, your life will be far less successful than it could be. This is the very reason so many people today are working harder, living poorer, and feeling time pressure. They allow urgent situations to dictate how their time is spent. The important situations go neglected. Sooner or later, these become both urgent and important. These people end up in a self-created crisis—a money crisis, a health crisis, a business crisis, or a family crisis. Most of these are preventable by choosing to spend your time doing what's important instead of overreacting to what's urgent. Learn that you are the sum of your choices and decisions. One of the most important choices you can make is to decide what's important. Then commit yourself to spending your time achieving important results, instead of responding to urgent but unimportant distractions. Procrastinating and getting ready to get ready is a major time thief for many entrepreneurs.

Now O'Clock!

Turning Time into Money Is a Predictable Three-Step Process

1. Start Your Mission by Deciding What Is Most Important

It is imperative that you create a mission and vision statement. If you don't know where you are going, how are you going to get there? This statement tells you what is most important. The purpose of your mission statement is to remind you of the values your enterprise is built on. Because time is your most valuable commodity, your time must be spent expressing your most important values. This assists you in turning time into money. Prospecting, recruiting, teaching, training, developing leaders, growth, change, and letting go are all simultaneously involved. You'll also begin to enjoy the process. This is why it is important you have a well-defined mission and vision for your enterprise. If you don't have a mission and vision statement, do it now. Once you have a clear picture of how you plan to create value for your customers and associates, and once you know precisely where you desire to go, you will begin to turn time into money.

2. Create a Game Plan for Results

Develop a plan of action and stick to the plan. Hold yourself accountable. Set specific goals and priorities. Develop a daily method of operation and put it on paper. If you are part-time, you should devote five to twenty hours of effort into your dream. Full-time would be thirty-plus hours. Know exactly what your plan is and follow through. Put your specific goals and actions onto paper. Go over it nightly to hold yourself accountable. This will assist you in staying on track. Chart your time. I ask my clients frequently to tell me what they did during the last few days. Very, very few can tell me what they did. This is the reason that you must put your game plan down on paper. Your self-management skills will greatly improve immediately. In the time you allot for yourself to propel you to your goals, do what is most productive and what will bring you the greatest results long-term. At least 80 percent of your time should be devoted to marketing your services in the early stages of your enterprise. Entrepreneurship requires momentum to create the compounded results. It's simple disciplines done consistently over a long period of time. Your weekly goal, part-time, is to find one new client per week to use your products and services. It sounds easy, but very few people ever do this consistently. This would be a total of fifty-two clients per year that you personally created—not counting what your organization produced. If you are full-time, you focus on two new people per week. This would give you 104 new clients per year that you personally created. This only happens with consistent effort, seven days per week over a period of time. It doesn't happen overnight. It is a process to collect the payoff. Don't seek perfection; seek effectiveness in what you do.

3. Develop New Thought Patterns and Creative Habits

The tapes you listen to, the books you read, and the people you associate with are all sources of new and useful ideas and ways of thinking. The people and situations will change as you change and begin hanging around with the right people, while detaching from the wrong ones. It's very difficult to soar with eagles when you roost on the ground with turkeys. Start studying successful people and watch what they do. Interview successful people whenever and wherever the opportunity presents itself. I have spent the last ten years pouring through my entire library of self-help, motivational, investing, financial, and spiritual books and tapes, and I have attended hundreds of seminars and workshops, all for the purpose of becoming a better person. I have learned to let go of old, limiting thoughts and doubts, I have forgiven myself for past failures and challenges, and, most of all, I have forgiven others who may have harmed me. The thoughts you think today will be a large part of what dictates your future. Developing good productive habits and patterns, and doing this in an efficient manner that takes the least amount of time and energy is the key to your future success.

Setting Your Goals and Establishing Your Whys

Your vision and mission statement will give you a view of your destination and a general picture of what you desire to achieve and become. Setting your goals and priorities is going to be very important especially when it comes to determining your priorities and immediate actions.

Set goals that are your own—not someone else's. It's your enterprise, your career, and your future. Take charge of it and do what is meaningful and best for you, both short-term and long-term. It's not selfish to think of yourself first. You are in the process of change, and as you change, you will be able to assist others with change also. Do not rely on the advice of your family and friends, unless they are already successful in what you are doing. Remember, your success is ultimately going to be up to you. The old adage, "If it's meant to be, it's up to me" applies here. Make sure to put your goals in writing; this increases clarity and commitment. Your goals should be challenging, yet attainable. Don't set a $500,000 a year goal if you've never made a penny before in the industry. Create goals that are reachable, while still being ones that you stretch to attain. Setting goals that are impossible cause most people to give up way too quickly. And when the goals are too easy, most people get bored. Worthwhile goals are the ones you can achieve by pushing yourself to perform better than you have previously. It's OK to think big, but you must act big, too. My father once said to me, "Son, it ain't braggin' if you can back it up." In free enterprise, as in almost anything, time will either expose you or promote you.

All goals must have deadlines. If there is no a target date for completion, it's not a goal, it's really just a daydream. You must have dreams and you must set goals, but what is much more important is to be a goal-getter, not a goal-setter.

As an entrepreneur, it works best when you monitor yourself and have performance or qualifying terms that will allow you to measure your progress. Remember: you are your own boss now! Your daily goals should have a performance indicator and criteria for success at the start of your endeavor. Major goals should be measurable, so that you have a way of keeping track of dollars per month, ninety days, six months, and one year. Keep records about your results, including the number of product testimonies, new clients, new positions or leadership positions attained, quality time set aside with family, children, or self, as well as specific goals to develop yourself by reading books and listening to audio programs.

Every major goal should have performance criteria for a particular success. If you are vague or unable to see what you desire to achieve, it isn't clear enough in your own mind to be a goal. Set your priorities to attain your most essential goals. Some goals are more important than others. Some you must do! Some you should do. List your goals in order of importance, and make sure you achieve them. Great time management means doing the difficult things first.

Turning time into money begins with investing a great deal in yourself and turning good time management into results. Always ask yourself this key question, "What did I do today that moved me closer to my goals or further from my goals?" A daily inventory like this lets you know how much progress you are really achieving. Most people value their time so little that when I ask them what they did two days ago in the 8:00 A.M. to 10:00 A.M. time slot, for example, they can't recall. Once again, successful people understand that time is their most valuable commodity, and they don't waste it; they make it work for them. I can recall what I do everyday because I know how to turn time into money. I keep a daily planner of all my activities. Before I go to bed, I list out everything that I will accomplish the following day. All of my appointments are listed in my calendar that I follow rigidly. I'm very thorough on my callbacks and follow-ups. I'm always preparing for upcoming events and speaking engagements.

As an entrepreneur, you should always have next week's leads in place and your ads placed. You should have a list of your organization

Check Out Receipt

Finney County Public Library
620-272-3680
http://www.finneylibrary.org

Sunday, August 19, 2018 3:55:44 PM
MOHAMED, HAMZE A

Item: 2008836
Title: Secrets of happy people : 50 techniqu
es to feel good
Material: Book
Due: 09/09/2018

Item: 568616
Title: Psychologically unemployable : life o
n your terms
Material: Book
Due: 09/09/2018

Total items: 2

"NEW LIBRARY HOURS"
Monday-Saturday 9:00am--8:00pm
Sunday 1:00pm--6:00pm

with phone numbers and e-mail addresses for speedy communication. It's now very effective to communicate with large and small groups via e-mail. It takes a concerted effort to effectively manage your time. Always be thinking to yourself, *How do I turn time into money? What can I do to improve my use of time?* Turning time into money begins with investing some time in thoughtful planning.

Over and over, I ask people to describe their goals and dreams. The standard knee-jerk reaction I often hear is a six-figure income, more freedom, or $25,000 or $50,000 a month. These are all good goals to shoot for, but how much time, energy, and action does it take to produce the results of your goals? What does it take to meet these large goals—what is your plan? It's OK to think big, but act big as well. How will you manage your time to meet these goals? What does it take in time and energy to achieve six figures or $250,000? Most people don't have a clue about how to plan in order to get from point A to point Z. Then they don't factor in how much return on time and energy it will take.

Most people spend their whole life getting ready to get ready, procrastinating throughout their entire life. I see people who think they are full-time, and who have actually quit their jobs to live their dream in free enterprise. I've seen people who couldn't wait to quit their jobs to go full-time, and then, when they actually quit, they devote less time full-time then they did part-time. Fear and old tapes of self-sabotage keep them from taking the proper action required to create the compounding effect of multiple results to meet their goals. The bottom line is planning to succeed, not planning to fail. Here are some questions to ask yourself in establishing your plans:

Marketing

Who are the potential customers that could benefit from your products and services, your leadership, your company, and your wisdom? Whom do you desire to attract? How many new customers and clients do you desire to create on a monthly average for the next two years?

Training

What kind of training will you provide? Your company's and your own? Do you have a strategy to introduce to the people on your team? What about books, tapes, and coaches?

Leads

If you don't have people to talk to, you are out of business, and you will definitely be getting ready to get ready. What is your budget for buying leads during the next ninety days or six months? No budget? Then make it happen! Advertise in the newspaper, warm market, cold market, Internet, magazine, postcards, Chamber of Commerce, and lead clubs. How do you learn to write ads? By doing!

Tools

Some tools you'll require include a telephone, headset, computer, website, tape recorder, voicemail, fax, digital cameras, printer, laptop, secretary and assistants, cell phone and email. It is essential that the bulk of your time is spent on revenue-producing activity (R.P.A.), on your most important goals that produce results, and on the most important items on your to-do list. Eighty percent of your effectiveness will come from achieving 20 percent of your goals. When you set goals and priorities and work on achieving the most important ones, you are focusing on the bottom line of getting results. This is when time becomes money! The more efficient you become, the more money you'll get for your time, and the sooner you own your own freedom. I have discovered a very important fact about time usage. In my early career, I spent most of my time in recurring patterns of behavior, without giving much thought to them. These were just old habits. Some were time-savers, while most were time-wasters—TV, gossip, politics, he said/she said, getting ready to get ready, procrastinating. I learned that this type of activity steals time from your life. The key to becoming efficient with time usage is to identify any time-wasting habits and replace them with ones that will help you turn time into money.

Find Out How You Spend Your Time

"Time will promote you or expose you."

Very few of my clients can recall by the hour what they did two days ago, except perhaps the hour they got up in the morning or went to bed at night. Time management is an area almost everyone can improve on, and a great place to start is to keep a time log for one week. This is a very simple task, but one that will be quite eye-opening for most everyone when done properly and honestly. It shocks most people to see how unproductive they are with their time.

Find out how much time you devote to your enterprise by writing down every activity you engage in and how long it takes. Keep track of how many messages you left, how many people you actually talked to, how many people you disqualified, how many nos and yeses you received. How much time was devoted to interviewing prospective clients and partners? How much time was spent listening to tapes? Did you attend any workshops or seminars? How many successful people did you interview? Keep track of each activity separately and write it all down for seven consecutive days. Then, keep track of time spent watching television, reading newspapers or magazines, and going to movies. How much phone interviewing and face-to-face interviewing did you do? How much time was spent on paperwork? Finding out how your time is actually being spent is a real eye-opener. We often don't realize the huge amount of time that is being spent on activities other than achieving the goals we set out to gain. We don't realize how little we know about managing our time and how easily time gets away from us. Most of us waste about half our time, and even the most effective people waste two hours a day on average.

Once you have completed how you've spent your time for one week, write your answers to the following questions:

- What were my greatest time-wasters?
- How much time is being wasted by repeated interruptions? Who or what is responsible for them? How can they be minimized?
- What do I do consistently that I think is urgent but is really unimportant?
- What are the least and most productive times of each day?
- Whom should I spend more time with? Whom should I spend less time with?
- To which activities should I be devoting more time?
- On which activities should I be spending less time?
- What patterns and bad habits are causing me to waste time?
- Am I trying to do too much?
- Am I procrastinating? Why?

Find a happy medium in learning how to turn time into money. None of us can do everything efficiently all the time. Learn to fail more intelligently, and don't take it personally. The key to turning time into money is simply having a well thought out plan and the simple discipline and commitment to work it every day. It means taking action even when you don't feel like it, realizing that now is the most important time, because now is the only time you have.

GETTING UNSTUCK
GETTING THROUGH BARRIERS TO CHANGE

Standing still—not moving, in a rut, going backward instead of forward, lost, mired, wallowing—all these phrases that mean the same thing: STUCK! This happens to many of us at one time or another in our lives. We want something; we'd love to be successful, rich, famous, wealthy, liked, loved, or popular, but we don't know how to get unstuck. Fear is usually the dominant element that keeps us stuck. We put off the action that will create our dreams, saying we'll do it tomorrow, next week, next month, or next year. Networking is the opportunity to win the game of your life on your terms and in your time frame. The future is now, and the future belongs to those who love, believe, and act on their dreams. People who are unstuck are people who take action, those who set and then achieve their goals. They are people who forgive themselves and others, people who know how to love themselves and others. These are people with heartfelt visionary leadership.

People who are stuck make goals and plans, but they put off the first step until tomorrow or next week or next year or until some future time when life is better. They make promises to stop drinking, quit smoking, spend more time with their family, pay off debt and credit card balances, begin exercising regularly, or become more assertive. They break these promises repeatedly and then feel guilty about their lack of resourcefulness.

They take no action in their enterprise. They take no action to prevent dire consequences to their health or well-being, despite repeated warnings from their doctor, family, and friends. They wait for a catastrophe, a sign, or an offer that is too good to be true—or until they absolutely, positively cannot take it anymore, before doing what they knew all along they should or could have done in the first place.

Being stuck is not a satisfying, comfortable place to be. When you are stuck, you do not feel good about yourself, and you do not think clearly.

You doubt your abilities, and you dislike yourself. Your self-esteem is usually low, and your confidence is not at its peak.

The information I will share with you about getting unstuck will assist you with psychological obstacles, emotional barriers, and practical considerations that stop you from moving forward to achieve your dreams. This is about moving through the blocks so you can change how you have been changing yourself.

The first step is moving out of denial. This is important, so you can be free to have peace of mind. If you insist that your current and persistent inaction will somehow get you where you want to go, you are fooling yourself. Getting unstuck gives you the opportunity to enjoy the life you deserve and desire!

If life and success are a journey, then being stuck is a detour. Many people get packed, but they never take the trip of their life. They sit on the bench, keep their foot on first , or watch from the sidelines— intellectualizing all of their reasons for being stuck while someone else is out there succeeding. Fear brings people to a standstill, and they wonder if they can continue the journey.

To truly understand getting stuck, you have to understand and identify the main reasons we all get stuck at one time or another.

- Low self-esteem
- Not seeing alternatives
- Not knowing what you really want
- Defending the status quo
- Fear
- Lack of cooperation
- Perfectionism
- Lack of will

When you are stuck, you tend to look at other people's lives with envy. You come to believe they have some special, magical, unattainable quality that allows them to get what they desire and deserve from life. You may think you can get unstuck, but you don't. You can, and some will! Done... Finished... Completed!

Why Change?

If you were to make a list of words easier said than done, *change* would top it. One syllable, six letters meaning "to alter, vary, or make different." The word change brings forth conflicting emotions for anyone who hears it. What happens when you think about change? What are the first words or images that come to mind? Most people view change as something that is chosen for them, not by them. Most people view change as a negative, not as a positive. Most people also view change as something painful. But for some, change may seem to be a reasonable, pleasurable proposition. What could be better than abandoning unhealthy habits, altering a bad relationship, changing dull, old routines, accepting new challenges, or working on change to improve the quality of your life? The results of change can only leave us better off than we were before. So why do we dread and fear change? What is the challenge with change? How did it get a bad reputation?

Many people fail to see the highly positive effects of change until they are forced to change because of some unforeseeable circumstance. This is what happened to me. I started having delirium tremors at age thirty-two. My drinking was completely out of control at this time, and I didn't believe I could ever stop. I visited a doctor, thinking I was having a heart attack. This was denial at its most extreme. He called an ambulance, and they took me to a four-day detoxification center and then to a thirty-day recovery center. I haven't had a drink since. I had to change or I was going to die. It was that simple for me. This was the first of many radical changes I have experienced in my life. This is how many people are forced into changing. Sometimes it is for the better. What it all boils down to is that I changed—not just my drinking habits, but the entire way I thought about everything.

I abandoned old habits, started resolving long-standing problems, improved my relationships, expanded my horizons, started attending seminars and workshops, started (and continue) to purchase and read hundreds of self-help and motivational books and tapes, mentored with successful six- and seven-figure income earners, and modeled myself after other successful people, I went through a series of setbacks while continuing to get back on my feet, and I changed how I viewed what almost everyone else would consider failures. To me, they were only part of my journey on the path to my promised land. I understood that my philosophy of life had to change, because I was way behind on my dreams. I started to view change differently and to look at the positive results it would bring me, instead of focusing on the "what if's" of change. Overreacting was always one of my danger zones, and I started to improve on that flaw. I started to understand that I couldn't change or control a lot of situations, but I could change how I viewed all of them. I realized I no longer had to be right all the time.

Psychological Myths About Change

When most of us change, we are likely to approach it in one or more of these ways:

1. **Scared Straight** – Shocked into change by illness, a near-death situation, or out-of-body experience. This is when people are scared "within an inch of their lives." This was me in 1988 with alcohol.

2. **Crying Uncle** – We all "cry uncle" eventually. We change our lives, our behaviors, and our attitudes because we can no longer endure the feelings or pay the emotional price of staying the way we are.

3. The Straw that Breaks the Camel's Back – This method is torturous. When you change in a burst of anger because you've experienced the proverbial straw that breaks the camel's back, you initially regret your decision, because it really wasn't a decision, it was really a reaction. You suffer through self-recrimination and wonder what you could have done differently before finally looking forward and improving your life.

4. Dreading the Alternative – This reason to change comes into play whenever you've trapped yourself in a corner. Your back is against the wall. You can no longer postpone, avoid, or resist change, because the very real consequence of staying the same will cause more distress than the imagined cost of conducting your life differently. You change to avoid the dreaded alternative.

5. Disaster Relief Because Life Is Too Short – Job layoffs, restructuring, buyouts, getting fired, natural disasters, divorces, aging parents who come to live with you, prolonged illnesses, and car accidents—life is full of unforeseen events. The only choice you have is to deal with the aftermath. How about working with a company that goes out of business, or a company that changes your pay plan? Perhaps you have been in a company where the top leaders left. Sometimes disasters force you to change, and other times a loss experienced by someone else forces you to change. For instance, someone you know has a health issue, and then gets a divorce. Your sympathy for this person leads you to realize that a similar misfortune could happen to you. "Life is too short," you think, and you take action to make the positive changes you were putting off for another day.

All of these approaches to change are effective. They are the reasons most of us finally get around to improving our lives. Unfortunately they also involve:

- Postponing, resisting, and avoiding change for as long as you possibly can—you refuse to change until not changing is intolerable. In the interim, considerable damage is done to yourself, other people, and your relationships.
- A precipitating event
- A tragedy, trauma, confirmation, or disaster must happen to you before you change. Your life improves but you believe change was not your choice. It was an inescapable reaction to circumstances beyond your control.
- Pain and suffering.

These approaches are generally and mistakenly assumed to be absolutely necessary anytime change occurs.

Misperceptions About Change

I am sure at some time in your life you have heard someone say, "You have to hit bottom before you can climb back to the top." This widely accepted misconception implies that you have to grovel, suffer, and lose all hope before you will be able to change to improve yourself and your life. This myth convinces you to wait until a situation is awful and intolerable before you do anything to make it better. Because we have such negative reactions to change, we often convince ourselves that "things really are not so bad," which serves as a ready and repetitive excuse not to change.

I have a pleasant surprise for you. Nowhere is it written that you must suffer terribly before you change. In many instances, suffering is not required at all, and you certainly do not have to endure prolonged pain, frustration, or uncertainty. Hitting bottom is what you make it. The bottom does not have to be the gutter or the coronary care unit. It does not have to be the welfare line or the psychiatric ward. Your own bottom is the place and the moment you decide that you deserve more—that you deserve to have better health, to be happier, to be more creative, successful, prosperous, or fulfilled than you already are. The bottom is when you want to get unstuck and viewed more favorably. To move forward, you have to hit your own bottom and be prepared to rise above it. You can choose to change, and you can begin whenever you please.

Why Change? This is a very interesting question. Perhaps a better statement would be, "What can you change that will most improve the quality of your life?"

Here are some good questions to answer and put on paper:

- What do I want to do with my life in the time I have left to live?
- What do I want to experience?
- What do I want to witness?
- What do I want to learn?
- What do I want to be a part of?
- What do I want to change, shape, and leave better than I found it?
- In short, what do I want to do for the rest of my life?
- Who do I want to impact and how do I want to impact them?
- What will I become?

These are great questions to ask yourself. If you have trouble answering any or all of these questions, then perhaps you are stuck. Most people don't like where they are in life, but they continue because it is comfortable and less scary than the unknown. I call this a miserable "comfortable" zone. Fear (once again, the great paralyzer of dreams) is what keeps most people from changing, and it is also what keeps most people from living their dreams.

Change may not be easy. Life's journey presents an endless array of choices and dilemmas that may distract you from the route you have chosen. That's why you must reach deep inside yourself for the force to propel you toward your goals. If you find that inner strength, you can leap the hurdle and surge ahead. If you come up empty-handed, you will give in to temptation or postpone the action you planned to take.

A Matter of Will

Every change contains its own moment of truth. Actually, every change contains many moments of truth—moments when you act upon your choices or do not act, when you move forward or turn back, when you take a step or postpone it. You may know what you really want and believe you deserve it. You may conquer fears and disarm your defenses. You may clear all other obstacles from your path. But when all is said and done, at a moment of truth, change becomes a matter of will.

You resolve to take your first step and stay on course. You exercise resolve so that you adopt a new behavior or way of living and stick with it over the long haul. You actively resolve to resist temptations to return to old habits. When it is far easier not to, resolve is what gets you to do what actually must be done.

What Is Resolve?

Resolve and will are the two, synonymous, invisible hands pushing you forward. They are like a jumper cable feeding power to a dead battery. Will is the commitment that turns a pipe dream into a plan. It supplies the energy to turn your visions into reality. Resolve is a fire burning inside you. With the combination of resolve and will, you ignite new fires and begin to change. Change begins in present moment consciousness. It begins in the now (now o'clock) with will (I will it to happen—I will overcome, I will live my dreams). With your will, you ignite the fires and begin new change efforts. You produce enough energy to stay with any course of action you choose. Without it, you give in, give up, procrastinate, and get stuck.

Resolve is the deciding factor each time you face a moment of truth, stopping you from slipping backward. A moment of truth arrives each time you feel an urge to return to old ways of thinking or acting. Old habits and behaviors offer comfort and escape when you are tired, lonely, angry, or sad. In trying times, it takes resolve to avoid going back to old behaviors and patterns.

Will assists you to stay on any new path you choose for yourself. New behaviors and new patterns that you adopt require discipline and perseverance. You will face your enemy many times. It is your will and your developed "why" that will keep you on the path and prevent you from falling off. You have to develop a will to win, to succeed, and to make the proper breakthroughs. You will require a resolve that nothing will stop you from your dream. It comes down to how badly you want it. Will you pay the price? That is the question I ask you, and only you can answer it. The will and the amount of change you go through will determine when you will get to your promised land!

GOALS VS. RESULTS

Write your goals down, put them on paper, visualize them, romance them, smell them, feel them, touch them, and believe in them. This is good standard information that we are taught when it comes to goal setting. This type of goal setting is practical and informational. My question is, if this information is correct, why do so few people reach and achieve their goals in life? Why is it that only 7 percent of America achieves a six-figure income? Why is it that only one-twentieth of one percent of the households in America has a net worth of one million dollars?

It is much more normal and accepted to be average than to be exceptional in our society. This is why each year on December 31st a large percentage of our nation sets new goals, resolutions, and declarations. Two very common goals are "I want to lose weight and make more money in the next year." Go to any health club in January, February, and March—they are usually crowded with people determined to make good on their New Year's resolutions—but go back in April, May, June, or any of the summer months, and you will notice a large drop off in attendance. The reason for the sudden decline is simply motivation. We are all motivated. We want more mores: more personal time, more money, more freedom, more family time, and more opportunities. We want, wish, like, hope, plan, need, and many other words that really mean, "I am not committed!"

Exceptional people understand that consistent effort over a period of time coupled with personal growth will create consistent results. They have a very precise, clear mental picture of where they are going on their journey to success. If you are striving to live an exceptional life rather than an average one, make your goals reachable and realistic, yet big enough that you have to stretch to reach them. Realize that the key to goal getting, the key to creating consistent results, requires self-motivation coupled with action.

Self-Motivation

What is self-motivation? Almost everyone has attended a workshop or rally where they were motivated and inspired by an energy level that became infectious because a large number of people were gathered in one place who were all excited about the same situation at the same time. What happens when you get back to your office, back to your desk, back to your corner of the world, and reality starts to kick back in? What happens when the phone is not magically ringing off the hook because people heard you were at that seminar or workshop? What happens when it seems like the only knock on your office door is from the bill collectors and the dream stealers? Getting motivated is great, but I teach my clients that it is self-motivation that will keep them in the game when it seems that the odds are stacked against them— when it seems like they can't give their product away, let alone find any new clients; when it looks like they might actually have to "get real, get a job, and stop chasing rainbows."

Self-motivation is the internal driving force that says, "I see this opportunity, and I will not be denied!" Self-motivation is the true fuel for your engine. It is the "why" behind the "how." You may find yourself motivated for short periods of time by other people or external stimuli, but it is the power within you that will be the driving force that allows you to achieve your dreams. When you are able to motivate yourself, when you believe in your reasons for becoming an entrepreneur, and you believe not only in your ability to succeed, but that you deserve to succeed, there is no person and there is no external situation or circumstance that can steal that knowledge or that take that burning desire away from you. This is what keeps you in the game when you face adversity, and this is what allows you to overcome seemingly impossible odds to enjoy what you do while you are living, rather than focusing on what job you do for a living.

Self-motivation is the number one key when it comes to achieving results, not just goal setting. As a personal success coach and mentor, I have had the privilege of personally coaching over fifteen hundred clients and devoting over eleven thousand hours to understanding why people do what they do and why they don't do what they set out to do. I see far too many people set huge goals as new entrepreneurs without really understanding what it will take to bring these aspirations to fruition. I am a big advocate of daring to step out of the box and dream big in any situation. Setting lofty goals is great! It's great to dream big, but to achieve your goals and create results, your action has to match your dream!

Action

Action is key number two. Action is simple discipline practiced over a period of time to create results. As entrepreneurs, we do not get paid for time; we get paid for results. If you have big dreams and lofty goals, and if you intend to create great results in your enterprise, then you must take action in direct proportion to the results you seek to achieve. When you are new and unskilled as an entrepreneur, your results are often intangible in the beginning, slowly becoming tangible (visible) over time. This is the phase where most people give up on their dreams if they don't see immediate results.

In order to become a successful entrepreneur, you have to be willing to give yourself room to succeed, not to fail. It typically takes the average person two to five years to get comfortable with a new process like entrepreneurship. For most individuals, it is unfamiliar, unknown, and a lot of time is spent in the land of "What if?" *What if I succeed? What if I fail? What if they laugh at me? What if it works? What if it doesn't? What if no one purchases my product or service? What if I go broke? What if my life changes? What if I can't pay my bills? What if I can't prospect? What if I'm not perfect? What if I don't know all the answers to my prospects' questions? What if my partner or spouse thinks this is a scam? What if I have to go get a job again?* Remember, there is never any reward without risk.

I suggest that you begin to break your goals down into bite-sized chunks rather than setting a giant goal that seems unattainable or insurmountable. I see so many "wannabe success seekers" set goals that are so big that they become excuses to procrastinate instead of produce results. Instead, set smaller goals for a day, a week, a month, and a quarter. I teach people how to goal get, not just goal set.

If your objective is to achieve a six-figure income this year, it is important to have a plan of action for how to get there. Break this goal down into the actions that, when performed daily, will create the six-figure income you seek. This means achieving an average of $277 a day in order to achieve a six-figure income in a 365-day period. If your objective is to achieve a seven-figure income this year, you will be required to achieve an average of $3000 a day within a 365-day period to achieve your objective. These are examples of breaking down a financial objective within a stated time frame. Also notice that these goals are based on an average daily achievement.

Take into account as you break down your goals that some days will be better than others. I suggest that you look at what average results repeated consistently over a set period of time would bring you the larger results you desire. Expecting each day to produce an exact return on your time will inevitably put you in a position to feel fantastic on the days your goals are met or exceeded and less than fantastic on the days where you come up short. Alternatively, looking at average results over a long period of time gives you more room to be resilient—to have low highs and high lows—to not get so extremely excited when you have a big day and not get extremely discouraged when you have a day that is less than desirable.

In a perfect world, the same effort each day would produce the exact same result, but reality will prove to you that this does not happen, even for the veteran entrepreneur. Over time, your averages will increase and become bigger numbers, but you will always have phenomenal days where your bank account seems to explode, and other days where the results you generate are intangible but no less important.

Keep goal setting simple and don't spend a lot of time writing down your goals. Start with a day, a week, and a month as opposed to a major lifetime objective. Instead, focus the greatest amount of your time and energy performing the actions that will bring the greatest return now. I call this "revenue-producing activity." Exceptional people understand that they get paid for results, not time. This principle of turning time into results is the key to becoming a successful entrepreneur.

Results

As an entrepreneur, it is the results you are able to produce that will begin to affect your present circumstances, as well as your future. Exceptional people spend the majority of their time focusing on the results they are seeking to produce, rather than on the goals they are seeking to one day achieve. Exceptional people understand that achieving consistent results will eventually bring their goals to fruition.

As I mentioned earlier, it is much more normal and accepted to be average than exceptional in our society. Are you modeling yourself and your activities based on an example you have received from an average person or an exceptional person? Do you have a role model you can mentor with as an entrepreneur? I was very fortunate to have had two very prosperous and entrepreneurial parents. I never heard "we can't afford it" while I was growing up. My father always had fabulous, first-class cars and extremely valuable collectibles. I received a very solid foundation from my parents that taught me how to create situations to have the best of any possession I desired to own. I learned to create situations where I could afford exactly what I desired and to collect and appreciate objects of value, so that I acquired assets instead of just more stuff.

This gave me the foundation to seek out mentors and coaches, people I could model myself and my enterprise after as I went through my journey. Even though I did not have the opportunity to meet, talk to, or personally consult with many of these people, I read their books, listened to their tapes, and read biographies about them written by other entrepreneurs. I immersed myself in learning how they operated differently than the status quo, because this was how they achieved results that were so phenomenally different than the average person's.

Results and success are like beauty; they will be different for everyone, and their true value will only be appreciated in the eye of the beholder. What results do you desire to achieve in the next day, the next week, and the next year? How about in this lifetime? Who is your coach? Who are your role models? Whose footsteps can you follow as a road map when you require guidance on your journey to freedom? Whose life skills can you learn from, emulate, duplicate, and improve upon with skills and ideas of your own?

Consistently producing results requires a different skill set and level of commitment than we are taught in our educational system. Consistently producing results requires that you become innovative, creative, solution-oriented, proactive, focused, and diligent. Most of all, this requires that you remain self-motivated over a long period of time.

Are you beginning to understand the difference between goals and results? Although setting goals for yourself is important, are you beginning to see why creating results is what will take you to your promised land? Are you beginning to see that it is your action fueled by your intention that will fuel your enterprise and create changes in your life? It is the action inspired by the goal, inspired by the intention that will produce your results. Invest some energy this year in finding entrepreneurs, life coaches, and mentors whose journeys inspire you. Find some people you feel connected to that you can mentor with and model yourself after. These can be speakers, authors, or trainers; they can be living or deceased—it does not matter. What matters is that you find someone who has achieved results similar to those you aspire to and begin learning as much as you can from them on your journey.

PART SIX

BECOMING

COMING INTO YOUR OWN WITH
CREATIVITY AND IDEAS

Breaking Through Barriers to Change

INNER KNOWING
USING ALL YOUR FACULTIES FOR PROSPERITY!

Trust...love...peace...deserve...prosperity...abundance—all tremendous words that only a few people are comfortable with, words that so many are very uncomfortable with speaking and thinking. Your inner knowing is where your true potential lies. This is the seat of your consciousness, your creativity, your insight, and your intuition. I am talking about using the science of the mind. Isn't it time, no matter what your age, that you discovered your own true identity? Isn't it time you expanded your own expectations? Isn't it time you found your purpose and actually became purpose-driven? I'm talking about living in present moment consciousness and starting to tap into your inner knowing. It is time to move beyond the intellectualism of old thought processes and move into this inner knowing.

Have you ever heard the old adage "The first voice you hear may be your own?" What this means is that you are usually right when you learn to trust your intuition. Have you been to a bookstore lately and noticed how much old wisdom is becoming very popular? This knowledge was handed down before TV, radio, computers, and modern technology. Many of you have read Florence Shinn (1925), Napoleon Hill (1937), and Dale Carnegie (1930s).

Socrates stated that the unexamined life is not worth living. And it's how we examine our life that determines its worth. Since the days of Socrates, our source of meaning and value has shifted from a unified social consciousness to an individual consciousness. Today we no longer depend on the society we live in to confer an identity that validates our existence. People are hungry today—hungrier than ever before. Folks, there is a shift going on and you are part of it. People are fed up with just getting by. Over half the people in America are looking for a way to change, make more income, and find spirituality. Look how packed Barnes and Noble or your local bookstores are on the weekend. Look at the large number of titles available in the self-help section, the religion section, and the new age section, as well as the recovery and relationship sections. People are waking up—and some are taking action.

Join the Revolution

There is a revolution going on. People are exploring their inner space and their acquisition of knowledge through their internal senses. People are changing; are you? Change how you pay attention; this is imperative to your future now. What you notice is determined by how your attention is organized. Growing up, we develop habits for placing our attention, and this in turn determines what we know. I have found that most people erroneously believe that attention is attracted by interest. However, our attention is more often attracted by our own inner state, and then we stay interested because of the way we have learned to place our attention. What this means is that most people intellectualize rather than internalize. They don't trust themselves. Once again, this is a self-esteem issue. Most people look for answers in all the wrong places instead of trusting their own internal self. They get advice from their peers, and for most people, these are absolutely the wrong people to get advice from. They seek acknowledgement and approval, even though the only person's approval required is their own.

We separate ourselves from our own internal communication by objectifying things in order to categorize and intellectualize them. We override the true signals of our body, our heart and mental imagery, creating doubt about our own internal experience. Clearly you must change for this to change. However, our culture has taught us to pay attention to our outer senses of seeing and hearing, with a tendency toward rational analysis.

There are many methods of developing the inner self, such as learning to read your own and other people's body signals, visualization, intuitive hunches, mentoring, affirmations, modeling, imagination, meditation, and infinite intelligence, just to name a few. Self-esteem, confidence, letting go of fears, forgiving your past and your past experiences, loving yourself, and getting in tune with the universe are other major areas where trust of self causes inner knowing to occur. The conscious thoughts that you have adopted hold your bank account of life at its present status.

The fabulous motivational speaker, Jim Rohn, talks about adopting a new philosophy. It is imperative that your philosophy of life is in tune with your dreams. You have heard me and many other leaders in life talk about raising your consciousness. "What does that mean?" you ask. "How do I do it? Who will teach me?" Until a few years ago, I myself knew nothing of consciousness, and I didn't even have a definition of what it meant. I will give you a definition in laymen's terms:

Consciousness is total knowledge of the universe, past, present, or future as it is at this moment. It's a belief that one knows all, and all knows one. Consciousness is the energy of deity, which creates and pervades all space; it's a sense of unity with the universe.

This is probably the best definition I have found to date. What does that definition mean to you? It's about having an awareness of who you are, where you are, where you have been, and where you are going. It's about unity with the universe. People that understand consciousness know without hesitation they were put here for a purpose.

How many of you know your purpose? I finally found mine after forty-one-and-a-half years on this planet. I was made aware that my purpose was to assist people with the way they think—to assist people to take off the shackles, the chains, and the ties that bind in order to free them from bondage, the same bondage I lived in for many years. I became a freedom fighter. I always thought that if I had enough money, I would automatically be happy. After I made and saved a lot of money, I found that money didn't buy me happiness. I was not miserable, but I knew there had to be more to happiness than money. I had to find my purpose.

This is the reason I started my own seminar company. It was a way to send my message to more people than I could by being a network marketer. My questions to you are, "Do you know your why? Do you know your purpose? Are you hungry for it? Are you striving, are you insatiable, or are you caught up in the day-to-day routine of just getting by or struggling to pay your bills?" I implore you to find a way to figure it out. It all starts with change. It's changing the way you think and act—adopting a new philosophy, reinventing yourself, moving into flow and out of resistance. Changing and growing, taking action and then learning from the actions you take. It's not "What did I lose?" but "What did I gain?"

I personally have invested over sixteen years in developing my own best human potential. I have read and reread hundreds of books, listened to tapes, attended seminars, rallies, conventions on personal growth, self-improvement, and personal development. All for one purpose—to be the best I can possibly be. Are you doing the same? My work in the last six years of consulting with over 1200 individuals, as well as with many small business owners and direct sales companies, has provided me with many insights into how to enhance each other's human potential and stimulate intuitive thinking.

One common assumption among the wide variety of people with whom I have worked is the perception that developing our innate human potential is a monumental, if not altogether very difficult task. This tells me that people resist change, even if it's for their own good. Some people have been offered reasons why they feel unable to develop their full potential. These perceptions create formidable barriers to the attainment of their creative dreams, goals, and ideas. Yet in spite of their initial resistance to developing their creative potential, most people with whom I have worked have learned a profound lesson: The barrier lies within their resistance, not within their innate capabilities. The key is to overcome the resistance you face and benefit from the experience that you work through. Success is a process, not a payoff, but you start to collect the payoff when you are in the process. It always comes down to paying a price. It's been said that you will pay $10 at the door on your journey to success, and there are no discounts on this journey.

Change Your Focus

Most people focus on what they get. It's not what you get that counts, but what you become. What are you becoming? Are you happy with your personal growth? Your results in life will have a direct reflection on the amount of personal growth you are accruing. What you speak, you become. Life is a self-fulfilling prophecy. The more credence you grant your limiting thoughts, the more they become your reality. Start to develop more creative thinking patterns—ones that focus you on your own inner wisdom. Use the God-given thoughts you have. Rely less on outside external communication and more on your internal communication.

We all have great minds; we all have untapped human potential. You do not have to be a genius to be successful. It is possible for almost anyone to experience creative breakthroughs. We all have a call to greatness. Most of you just haven't recognized it or just flat out don't believe you have it in you. Greatness, just like prosperity, is a state of mind. Success is an attitude. It is peace, love, harmony, calm, excitement, belief, vision, prosperity, and it is an inside job—an inner knowing that permeates within you. A saying I like to use is "Dig your well before you are thirsty." Another one I read just this week is "It doesn't matter if the horse is blind; just load the wagon." In essence, you must know you are successful before the physical action even begins. Success is an inside job.

I have devoted my life to discovering the answers of inner knowing. What I am finding is: one after another, the greatest writers, poets, artists, speakers, and athletes all say that it takes more than talent. The underlying theme is that their greatest work comes to them from beyond the threshold of consciousness. Napoleon Hill called it infinite intelligence in his 1937 classic, *Think and Grow Rich.* How many of you have read the book? How many have read it more than ten times?

When you understand this wisdom, it is a great force. Many of us spend a good part of our life in resistance, following the status quo of life, plodding along in struggle mentality. Infinite intelligence is God energy; it's the wisdom of the universe. Whatever term you use, they are all applicable; they all mean a higher creative power that you work through. I call mine God! One of the best ways I have seen it described is by Aristotle. He called it: Discovering Universal Truth.

Four Ways to Discover Truth:

1. Scientific Reasoning – using experimentation to create and test hypotheses
2. Practical Reasoning – using practical reasoning and common sense
3. Philosophical Reasoning – using logical argumentation and reasoning
4. Intuitive Reasoning – the direct intuitive apprehension of truth

Aristotle maintained that, while any of the first three can lead us to truth, intuitive reasoning—because it is the direct apprehension of truth and not subject to potentially faulty logic or reasoning—was the only means to reach universal truths (truths that exist outside human logic and reasoning, truths sought by the great minds).

Many people today refer to this as "tapping in." In my sixteen years of entrepreneurship and public speaking, I have met and worked with many great minds. I noticed that many of them seemed to believe that they had the secrets, and that everyone wanted to know those key few ingredients. The script, the special leads list, the special tapes, that one special gold nugget—if only they could get their hands on it, the key would turn. Because of my success, many people ask me, "What do you say when they say such and such?" Saying the right thing is not the secret. The real secret is the process and learning from it. Creatively productive people consistently develop and use techniques to spur greater creative thinking to develop their highest mental and spiritual potential. Great minds lead themselves out of their local logical mind in order to receive input from the universal mind: infinite intelligence.

Jan Ehrenwald wrote in *Anatomy of Genius,* "Genius is not a function of genes or hormonal influence; genius is Process." It is correlated to the individual's life cycle. Genius is dependent upon what the individual is doing or is determined to do with his or her original gifts.

Eastern masters tell anyone seeking wisdom or enlightenment, "The journey is the goal." In other words, the process of seeking wisdom is as valuable as any wisdom that we can obtain through our search. If you desire to understand wisdom from great minds, realize that the actual process you use to discover their ideas and your personal journey will be as important as any wisdom you encounter. The key is to tap into your own inner knowing and intuition. Get out of your logical mind; trust and believe in yourself and your journey. In the process, you will find your purpose; you will find your why.

IDENTITY
DEFINING WHO YOU ARE

Defining your identity will keep you focused as you set priorities, organize tasks, deal with emergencies, and accomplish challenges in your personal and business life. If you have no concept of your identity, you run the risk of trying to be everything and do everything in a random and haphazard way.

Who Are You?

Defining your personal identity involves self-awareness— understanding who you currently are, as well as who you want to become. Taking inventory of yourself can be an uncomfortable and sometimes painful experience, but it is necessary if you want to improve. In this chapter, I'm going to ask you to consider some intensely personal issues so you can make the changes you are looking for.

You are a limitless being with capabilities that you are probably not aware of and have never used. Take the questions in this chapter to free yourself from the limiting aspects of your own self-image. Just as you don't become a millionaire and then start thinking like one, it is impossible to outperform your own self-image.

Getting to know yourself well is an extremely important process, leading to your ultimate happiness and success in both your personal and professional life.

Self Inventory

- Describe your predominate attitude about yourself, about your life, and where you are going.
- Describe your self-image.
- Describe how you treat other people.

In answering these questions, avoid:
- Defining yourself in terms of external things
- Defining yourself in terms of "should's"
- Defining yourself in terms of a stereotypical role
- Comparing yourself too harshly to other successful people

Describe Your Identity
- How do you spend your time in your business or company?
- What are your team's strengths?
- What are your greatest challenges?
- Are your skills being fully utilized?
- Do you like your present status in the company?

Redrawing Your Identity Map!
Ask yourself and write down the answers to these questions:

- How do you feel about yourself?
- How do people treat you in business and out of business?
- How do you spend your time in your business?
- What do you do when you are not working or creating?
- What are your strengths?
- What are your weaknesses?
- What are you doing to improve yourself?
- How fast are you willing to change?
- How badly do you want success?
- Do you love yourself? Do you deserve to have it all?
- Do you have a plan? Do you work your plan?

Make a Decision to Change and Reinvent Your Identity
The following powerful suggestions for change from Jim Rohn have helped me a great deal on many occasions:

- Do you view change as positive or negative? How do you react to change?
- What fears are holding you back today?
- Are you dedicated to change or to staying in the comfort zone?
- What risks do you take? Growth involves risk—if you risk nothing, you get nothing.
- Focus on what you will become, not what you get. Success is a process, not a payoff.

The Three Key Characteristics of Change

- Change is constant and unavoidable
- Change creates fear
- People tend to resist change

Change threatens your sense of security. Even people who are struggling resist change. Your survival and that of your organization or business is directly related to your ability to adapt to change.

Two Ways to View Change

Most people's first reaction to change is fear based and danger oriented. They avoid change; they fear it and attack it. A smaller percentage view change as an opportunity; they accept it and acknowledge its uncertainty. This group lives in the solution; the first group lives in the problem.

When will you create your new identity? When will you decide to change?

GET IN THE GAME AND STAY IN THE GAME

As a personal success coach and mentor to entrepreneurs from all walks of life, I have had the privilege of spending thousands of hours with clients who are just getting started in free enterprise as well as those who have been in numerous entrepreneurial endeavors. I have coached people who have achieved no money, people who have achieved millions, people who have gone from zero to hero, and people who have struggled to just "make ends meet" yet who refuse to go back to the j-o-b and corporate America. I have coached professional athletes, actresses, movie producers, and stay-at-home moms. I have a very diverse client base, but one situation all of these people have in common is that they have had to "GIG"—Get In the Game—in order to begin realizing success as an entrepreneur.

Getting in the game means making a decision that you will not settle for living an average life in someone else's dream, because you are going to create an exceptional life by living your own dreams. As I stated in the previous chapter, making a decision is the greatest challenge for most people. If you are going to succeed as an entrepreneur, you will be required to make multiple decisions every day. I believe that most people avoid making decisions because they do not want to be held responsible for the resulting situation. Most people associate responsibility with a negative outcome, but in reality, claiming responsibility leads to both positive and empowering results.

Take a Chance and Participate

In many of my one-day workshops, I play a game with money. I stand on the edge of the stage, holding up a one hundred-dollar bill, and I ask, "Who is responsible for this?" At every event, the first reaction of my entire audience is to freeze. Everyone looks at each other, waiting for someone to react, wondering what to do next. I repeat the question until a few people begin to say "I am." I nod my head and keep repeating the question. Eventually, one person finds some courage and begins to move toward the stage, which then allows about four other people to get into action. Suddenly, all four are racing toward me, each more anxious than the others to claim responsibility. In the end, one person reaches me first, takes the "C-note" from my hand and claims responsibility. The result is the easiest hundred dollars ever achieved in the five-second journey from chair to stage.

My point here is that making decisions will require you to get comfortable with the idea of being responsible for both the desirable and less-desirable outcomes your decisions create. Realize that your decisions do not have to be perfect. In five years, you will probably look back at many of the decisions you make today and think, *If I knew then what I know now, I would have decided differently.* This is true for all of us, no matter what our vocation. What matters to you now, as you begin to claim your destiny and take back control of your present, is that you decide to get in the game and make the best decisions you are capable of, knowing that you have many great lessons ahead of you and that you are on your way to manifesting your vision.

Participation Makes a Difference

Getting in the game means being committed to learning a new set of life skills that will allow you to hone your craft so that you can get paid what the free market bears for the value and service you bring to the marketplace. It means becoming comfortable with the knowledge that success is a process and having the courage, the guts, and the intestinal fortitude to dive into that process each day, leading with your heart, knowing that the lessons you learn will prove invaluable in a future situation. Each day, you have an opportunity to grow from the people you meet, the situations you encounter, the lessons you learn, the challenges you turn into triumphs, and the risks that you take to earn the rewards you seek. The game of free enterprise and entrepreneurship is really the game of your life, and the question is: "Are you ready to play?"

Are you ready to start? When the whistle blows, will you be ready to take off from the starting line, or will you be sitting on the bench, tying your shoes? Are you ready to get in the game of free enterprise? If so, you are playing for high stakes—your freedom, your dreams, and life on your terms. Getting in the game means being committed to making short-term sacrifices to achieve long-term goals. It means learning to be consistent and diligent, and it means being rewarded for your efforts based on what you decide your time and energy is worth, instead of on what someone else is willing to pay you to complete a task on a job.

Getting in the game means allowing yourself to have dreams and visions of what your future will hold and then using your creativity to turn your ideas into results that will allow you to manifest your dreams. You might say, "But what if I am not creative?" Each and every person has creativity inside of them. Each and every child used crayons, pencils, and markers to make pictures at some point in their childhood. Perhaps you are not a great artist, but you have creativity!

What happens to most people in our society is that at some point during their childhood they are criticized by a teacher, a parent, or a peer, and they end up stuffing their creative impulses down inside in an effort to avoid humiliation. Your creativity is your uniqueness; it is what makes you different than everyone else. It is intrinsic to you—no one else will ever be able to duplicate it, and this is the value you bring to the marketplace. This is the value that, if you have the guts to reveal it, I guarantee that you will find a market for it. The process here is to take your vision, your idea, what you can see in your "mind's eye," and create a tangible product or service that will allow you to receive results in exchange.

I say results, because not everyone is in the game for money— although on my journey I have found that while "love makes the world go 'round," money pays for the trip! Whatever results you are seeking on your journey, the game is taking your ideas and creating a product or service that becomes valuable to the marketplace, and from there it is an experiment to see what value the free market will bear in exchange.

Stay In the Game

Once you have made the decision to get in the game, you will find that to "SIG"—Stay In the Game—will require a different set of habits than those that serve you in a typical job. Remember, this is the game of your life! Begin creating million dollar habits and you will greatly increase your odds of succeeding. Begin studying millionaires to see what they do with their time. You will find that almost every millionaire you meet has developed great habits to enhance the skills that have allowed them to achieve the level of success that they are achieving.

Entrepreneurship will require you to learn a whole new set of life skills, because in this industry you get paid for your results, not for your time. We as a society are conditioned to be hourly employees and are generally conditioned to create very few results in a short period of time on a job, because we get paid for the time we work, not the results we produce. Free enterprise works in exactly the opposite way. The free market will often pay you more for an idea or result that you create in an instant than for a project that you sweat and toil over and brainstorm and plan and perfect and get ready to do. Having said this, I will also tell you from my own personal experience that I have yet to meet an exceptional entrepreneur who has not developed a routine to focus the direction of their ideas and enterprise. Successful entrepreneurs develop simple, effective routines that they are able to commit to repeating day in and day out over a long enough period of time to begin to experience quantum returns on their continual efforts.

Schedule for Results

Here is example of a typical day in my life: I wake up at 5:30 am and spend about 30 minutes quietly meditating and creating my day in my mind's eye. I believe that in life we receive exactly what we expect, and since I expect to have an outstanding day every day, I spend this time focusing on exactly what I will accomplish in the next twenty-four hours. At 6:00 am, I get up and read the Sports section of the newspaper. Then I leave my home at 6:15 am for a three-mile power walk, after which I return home and take a ten-minute steam. I begin my work day with my first coaching client at 7:00 am. I spend the next six hours coaching one client each hour by telephone until 1:00 PM. From 1:00 PM to 4:00 PM, I eat lunch with my wife, we walk our three Jack Russell Terriers, I catch up on phone calls, meet with our two assistants, address any challenges, make a few prospecting calls, take another ten-minute steam, and at 4:00 PM I begin coaching again. I coach from 4:00 PM until 6:00 PM, and regularly I am scheduled as a guest speaker on one to two conference calls each night, in addition to my own call each Tuesday night at 7:30 PST (which I have conducted each and every week for almost seven years). After my conference calls, my wife and I process and pack any orders, I return phone calls, I prepare for the following day, I read self-help and motivational material, I rest for four to five hours, and then I wake up and repeat this schedule the next day. I repeat this routine Monday through Thursday. Friday morning, my limousine service picks me up between 3:30–4:30 am, and I leave to travel and speak at events and workshops.

This may seem like an overwhelming schedule, but understand that I have been conditioning myself to this routine for over seven years. I also love what I do, and it is so much fun for me that I am able to do lots of it without feeling pressured or bored, or like I "have to" stick to this schedule. This schedule is simply an example of several habits I have incorporated to create the success I am currently experiencing: multiple and consistent years achieving seven-figure incomes doing exactly what I have always dreamed of. Your habits will probably be different than mine, and all that is important is that you develop a routine that allows you to move toward your goals each day, a routine that promotes you and your enterprise. Begin to develop habits that are simple, easy, and fun so that you enjoy committing to them.

Success Habits

Create more value for yourself in time instead of focusing on time management.

Learn to spend your time in revenue-producing activity. I see so many people spending vast amounts of time getting ready to be productive. They organize their desks; they do their laundry, clean their kitchens, call their friends, ask advice, seek permission, and any number of situations to avoid doing the activity that will ultimately pay them in their enterprise. In each day, there are 86, 400 seconds and 1440 minutes, and once they are gone, they are gone! Carpe Diem! Seize the day! Seize the moment! There is a time for all of the activities I mentioned, but that time is early in the morning or late at night. Successful entrepreneurs spend the majority of their time connecting with people, prospecting for new business, asking for referrals, marketing their products and services—in other words, in revenue-producing activities. If you wait until your life is perfect to get started, I guarantee you will never start. Get in the game! If you were in the game, creating $200 of value for each hour of your time, forty hours a week, you could hire people to clean your office, do your laundry, wash your car, etc. You would be achieving $8,000 per week—that's $32,000 per month. Are you beginning to see why it is so important that you learn to focus on revenue-producing activities?

Begin Creating Opportunities Instead of Waiting for Them

It is imperative to your success in your entrepreneurial endeavor that you begin to create your own opportunities to connect with people and to create business instead of waiting for great people and sales to find you. A client recently contacted my wife Erica, a client who has attended many of my workshops and who has met and connected with many, many great entrepreneurs in the three years since I met her. She asked if any of our Breakthroughs to Success graduates had created a Mastermind group, because she was seeking one and had not yet attracted a group to collaborate with. My wife suggested that she call some of the people she has met at our events and invite them to Mastermind with her. Erica told her that if she has not yet *attracted* the situation she seeks, she might consider *creating* it instead!

If you spend your entrepreneurial career waiting for great opportunities and people to find you, you may find that you spend a great deal of time unsatisfied. The people you see who attract people, situations, and sales seemingly effortlessly have usually been in the game developing their skills and honing their craft for quite some time. They have created a network and can rely of referrals to sustain their enterprise.

In the beginning of your journey, it is imperative to your success that you take proactive action to create the results you seek. If a situation you desire to participate in or a contact you would like to make is not finding you, then consider investing the time and energy required to create it yourself! Remember though, simply stating your intention is not enough to create reality. Intention fueled by action will bring results!

Take Calculated Risks

This means risk for reward—have the guts to step into an opportunity with a specific outcome in your "mind's eye." This is a term I often use; it means the picture or image of what you desire that you can see in the back of your mind or behind your eyelids when you envision what you desire. Great entrepreneurs are constantly taking calculated risks to achieve their dreams.

A calculated risk means knowing exactly what the margin for error in any one venture is and being in a position to be able to withstand that margin if the venture should go in the tank. A calculated risk may be assisting a business partner to invest based on the margin for profit should the investment prove successful, while also having the knowledge that this business partner has invested in several such ventures and has always emerged victorious. Taking a calculated risk means investing only that which you can live and prosper without. It means that if you are rewarded for the risk you have taken, you will be ahead in the game of life, but also if the reward never occurs, you will not have spent your "last nickel" in a desperate act to "cash in big."

Eliminate Chaos: Peace = Profit!

Chaos could be named the number one sabotage of an earnest entrepreneur's dreams. Chaos can manifest externally in the clutter of papers in your office, the collage of Post-It-Notes slapped around your computer monitor, the stacks of files between your desk and the doorway, and the general conglomeration of "stuff" waiting to be addressed that keeps you from seeing the top of your desk or even your office floor on a daily basis. Chaos also often manifests internally in the form of being involved in company politics, the need to be right, overreacting to minor situations, proving your position, and justifying your actions or inaction.

Begin creating more room in your daily life for peace. Begin by taking ten minutes each day to organize your office first thing in the morning and again right before you turn off the lights for the day. You will be amazed at how much organization can be achieved in just ten minutes! Allow yourself to discard any old paperwork or messages that are no longer of relevance. A good rule of thumb is if you haven't required the information in thirty days, it can go in your round file, the wastebasket. An exception to this rule is business cards. I create stacks of business cards, organized by type of businesses, and use a rubber band to hold each stack together. I use the back of one drawer in my desk to store the stack. In my opinion, each card represents a connection, one that could prove invaluable in the right situation.

Begin creating more room in your daily consciousness for peace by extracting yourself from situations that consume your energy but offer no return. Company politics are a great example of this. Any type of politics can suck you in and drain the life out of you, and I have never heard of anyone creating wealth by being the person who is the shoulder to cry on for the other people in their life who are enmeshed in the drama. It's time now for you to drop the drama and move on to the task at hand—the juice, the fuel, your why, the energy that drives your bus. It is time to begin simply doing what is best for you and to stop spending tremendous amounts of time rationalizing, explaining, validating, justifying, philosophizing, pontificating, and proving your position to other people. If a decision feels right and you are within your own integrity, just make it and move on. Your own permission is the only permission you will ever require to make it in your own enterprise. Isn't having the ability and creating the freedom to make your own decisions the whole point of being an entrepreneur anyway?

I guarantee the more peace you are able to create in your consciousness and in your life, the more other people will want to be a part of your enterprise. This is why I say peace = profit! You can profit both monetarily and spiritually by eliminating the chaos that keeps you stuck in a position that is no longer comfortable. But remember, peace, like success, is a process, not a payoff. It is also like beauty—it will appear different to each individual, just like beauty is in the eye of the beholder. Your own peace and personal profit is yours and yours alone, not to be measured against what you perceive someone else is achieving. You will never know all of the ups and downs and in and outs of someone else's life and journey. Learn to judge your progress against your own personal benchmarks, and I guarantee you will find more fulfillment and satisfaction than you ever could attempting to compete with anyone else.

Become Proactive instead of Reactive

What is the difference between being proactive versus reactive? When you are reactive, you wait for a situation to dictate your behavior. Most people typically wait until a situation is out of their control, remain focused on the problem or challenge that created the situation, and then react to the situation from a position of stress and emotional upset.

As an entrepreneur, the key to changing the quality of your life is creating change in your life. If your desire is to be free to design the life you are living, then you will be required to spend your time living in the solution, not the problem. Living in the solution when you are facing adversity really means being proactive. When you are proactive, you make decisions about a situation in anticipation of the result you desire to create. Instead of spending a lot of time focusing on the problem, analyzing how it happened, why it happened, and how you could have avoided it, you immediately focus on achieving the best outcome possible.

As you spend more time in free enterprise studying the art of entrepreneurship, take notice of the challenges that arise and how quickly you are able to resolve them. I guarantee that if you focus on solutions instead of analyzing problems, you will learn to neutralize the chaos and drama, calm your racing heart, stay out of fight-or-flight reactions, and be more productive in time.

Most people waste a lot of time in their lives and enterprises by waiting for a situation or event to dictate their response. Almost always, the situations that we face every day that seem enormous and overwhelming can be minimized and neutralized if they are addressed sooner rather than later with a specific desired outcome in mind.

GROW AND GLOW
WHAT IT TAKES TO BE A WINNER

Have you ever wondered what determines a winner from a loser? The Stanford Research Institute conducted a study that concluded that 12 percent of our success depends on knowledge and technical skills and 88 percent depends on our ability to manage interpersonal relationships successfully. This implies a positive attitude, cooperation, enthusiasm, and commitment.

Talent is easily purchased. Think of the great athletes who never make it to the major leagues. Look at the talented actresses, accountants, students who would like to enter medical school, teachers who want to teach, and a host of others who are refused admittance into their preferred fields. You see, talent is not so expensive.

Education is also relatively inexpensive. It is easier to become educated in America today than ever before. You can obtain college degrees through the mail or from online courses. Student loans grant scholarships, and part-time jobs are available for people who really desire an education.

There is one thing that can't be bought, and that is attitude. Are you a winner or a whiner? A champ or a chump? Winners believe that something good will happen every time. I hear this in a winner's voice, and I see this in their body language. Your prospecting efforts are best thought of as sorting out the winners from the whiners, the champs from the chumps. As a professional sorter, you start to look for clues to make the accurate identification. Winners believe that everything happens for a reason. Ask yourself what good can come out of any challenging situation. One man sees a failure, a disaster, a catastrophe, a loss, a ruin, a bankruptcy, a suicide, an end, a tornado, a wreck, a hurricane, it's over, and sees no way out of it. Another man sees an opportunity to start over, to strive to accomplish, to build, to create, to develop, to flourish, to prosper, to flower, to germinate, to grow. The events matter far less than the meaning you give to them.

Remember that fear is faith turned inside out. What do you choose? One percent doubt does not equal 100% faith. You can think or wish about it, or you can believe and act on it.

Napoleon Hill stated: "Every adversity contains the seed of an equivalent or greater benefit." Thus, obstacles are a winner's stepping-stones to greatness. I once heard the story of a man named Walter Henly. He was whistling in an elevator. A rather sour woman in the elevator asked him what he was smiling and whistling about. He smiled and replied, "I have never liked this day before."

Someone once said that all men are created equal. I believe it is what they do with the gifts received at their creation that makes the difference. An individual's attitude determines to what extent he will develop his talents and in which direction he points his life. I've always been impressed by the philosophy of Oliver Wendell Holmes, who said "The most important thing about a person is not where he stands, but in which direction he is moving."

Success depends on a positive, persistent attitude. A winner closes the door on past failures. By viewing temporary setbacks as stepping-stones rather than stumbling blocks, we can build the kind of personal future that will be satisfying and rewarding. It's what we bring to life, not what life brings to us that counts. A winner knows that his attitude about losing determines how long it will take to win.

Life is too precious to take for granted. What is your view on life? Is it a struggle, or are you winning the game of your life?

Living in the Now

What time is it? Now o'clock! "One day at a time" is a phrase heard frequently by people familiar with 12-step programs. How many of you actually live with that attitude? Many people spend a lot of time dwelling on the past, or full of worry, fear, or dread at what the future holds.

Too many people reside in poverty consciousness: worrying about bills, debt, health, and the future.

As a personal coach, mentor, and success teacher, as well as a recovering alcoholic, I am someone who has been there, too. I have discovered that about 90 percent of all our problems could be eradicated by simply "taking no thought for the morrow." This saying is so simple, and yet so very profound. "When we look back in our mind, we allow what we see or think we see to cause us to feel feelings that no longer exist." (Think about this sentence again as you reread it.)

Our memories of the past contain images and glimpses of reality that are really no longer relevant to where we are right now in our lives. It may be important to look back in time to our family of origin to truly understand why we act as we do. But once we have looked and understood, we must burn the film and go on with our life. People who continuously live in the past spend so much wasted energy focusing on what they cannot change. They tell the same story over and over. "How do I forgive myself?" they ask, telling themselves, "I can't," or "It's not working." "You just do it" is the answer—forgive the past and move on.

Just as our memories play tricks on us so that we often only remember the hurts rather than the good moments, such a distorted focus prevents us from loving our lives, and this continues until we live for today. Learn to live in the moment. Live in the now. This is what I call present moment consciousness. Many people drag the past into the present, and that clouds their view of the future. This causes lack of self-esteem and keeps people from ever gaining the confidence they desire. What is your view of yourself? How do you feel about you? Do you deserve to have it all? Do you love yourself?

A similar kind of distortion can happen to someone who is always living in the future. This kind of person is easy to spot because they are always talking about what they are going to do next month and next year. This future-oriented person always says when such and such happens, then as a result, they will do such and such. There is nothing wrong with having dreams, plans, or goals, but a vision without an action plan won't get you very far.

To make the personal breakthroughs that really matter requires living in now time. Now time is real time.

Here are the changes you will start to integrate:

1. Develop present time consciousness.
2. The time is now o'clock.
3. Create a game plan—plan of action.
4. Have a daily method of operation.
5. Hold yourself accountable.
6. Work goals in small or short increments.
7. Break down issues to workable details.
8. How many do I have to talk to?
9. How many Nos?
10. How many sales?
11. Invest in books, tapes, seminars, modeling, mentoring.
12. Ask for the sale.
13. Become a student of the game, the company, the product, and the industry.
14. Learn all of the little things so you can teach all of them.
15. Evaluate what your time is worth.
16. Increase the value of your time.
17. To get paid more, you must become more valuable.
18. You don't get paid for time; you get paid for results.
19. A consistent game plan will produce consistent results.
20. Refuse to quit before your time.
21. Raise the bar—readjust your goals.
22. Your thought process determines your bank account; take it to the bank.

23. Become the driver, not the driven.

Always remember that no matter what has happened in the past, it has absolutely nothing to do with what's happing now or what will happen in the future, unless you believe that it does! Incorporate these powerful statements of resourcefulness into your thinking every day.

- I will give you inspiration; you must provide the perspiration.
- May your dreams be your only boundaries.
- "The future belongs to those who believe in the beauty of their dreams" (Eleanor Roosevelt).
- Life is a self-fulfilling prophecy.
- We are what we imagine, and that we become.
- We all move in the direction of our present dominant thoughts.
- To actualize, you must visualize.
- A burning desire is much more important than facts, numbers, or knowledge.
- The material items you earn or achieve are not nearly as important as what you become in the process of reaching your goals.
- "Nothing is so powerful as an idea whose time has come"—(Victor Hugo).
- You can't always control what happens, but you can control how you react.
- Wise advice from Lord Chesterfield when his son asked him, "How can I make people like me?" "My son," Chesterfield explained, "make other people like themselves a little better and I promise you this, they will like you very much."
- Treat others the way you deserve to be treated.
- You can tell a great man by the way he treats little people or a brand-new person.

- You have to prepare yourself to be successful, even though it may appear that you are struggling. It is like this: readiness for opportunity makes for success.

Winners see a pessimist as one who feels bad when he feels good for fear he'll feel worse when he feels better.

A real winner is someone who makes winners out of others. Learn to see issues from other people's vantage points in order to project this kind of attitude. You can be self-centered or others centered—which do you choose?

I recently read the book *Why Winners Win* by Art Garner. He talks about a common denominator that was found in 100 self-made millionaires. The common characteristic among them was that they were all "good finders." This means they had the ability to find something good in every person and in every situation they encountered. This was a group that ranged in age from twenty-one to seventy and whose educational backgrounds went from a third grade education to PhDs. These real winners in life develop a habit of practicing it over and over until it becomes permanently installed in their unconscious minds. At this point, they have programmed themselves to look for the good things in people and in situations.

The Importance of Focus

Working on all these areas at once with a plan of action will create momentum. Focus on what you want. If you don't know what you want, then decide what you don't want. Be fit emotionally—most people are out of shape emotionally. To strengthen your resolve, you have to have a plan that moves the pendulum, not just swings the pendulum.

Things happen for a reason. One day, I planned to watch a football game. The game was blacked out, so I watched an infomercial on personal power with Tony Robbins where I gained something very useful. The winner sees such events as synchronicity—the result of an unconscious positive intention. Losers view them as random good fortune, having nothing to do with them.

At the end of each day, you should play back the tapes of your performance. The results either applaud you or prod you to improve.

Don't Stop Here

In the pages that follow, there are many ways to continue the journey, ranging from FREE teleconference training to two-and-a-half day seminars, one-on-one mentoring to high quality, best-selling books and audio programs.

Jeffery Combs

Jeffery Combs, President of Golden Mastermind Seminars, Inc. is an internationally recognized speaker, trainer, and author, specializing in prospecting, leadership, personal breakthroughs, prosperity consciousness, spiritual enlightenment, mindset training, and effective marketing. His training revolves around personal growth and development, cuts to the chase, and delivers information that makes an immediate impact on your success!

Jeff is the author of the highly inspiring book and audio series, *More Heart Than Talent*, along with numerous of other motivational and personal development products. He has personally consulted with thousands of clients in his coaching career, and is committed to assisting people change the way they feel in order to achieve their goals and dreams.

Jeff is available for consulting, mentoring, and personal one on one coaching. His professional guidance will assist you to create maximum results now!

For further information, please call 800-595-6632 or visit his web site at www.GoldenMastermind.com

Golden Mastermind Seminars, Inc.

President & CEO of Golden Mastermind Seminars, Inc.

Internationally recognized trainer in the network marketing & direct sales industry and keynote speaker

Has personally coached and consulted with thousands of entrepreneurs and industry leaders since retiring as a ten-year veteran marketer

Committed to assisting people to change the way they feel in order to achieve their goals and dreams

Specializes in a 2-1/2 day workshop called Breakthroughs to Success! This is an absolute must for anyone desiring to go to the next level

Jeffery Combs

FREE

"More Heart Than Talent"
Teleconference training call
with Erica & Jeffery Combs
every Tuesday night

Time: 10:30 pm EST
Call: 212-461-5860 / PIN 7707#

800-595-6632
www.GoldenMastermind.com

GOLDEN MASTERMIND SEMINARS, INC.
THE MASTERMIND LIBRARY

With over 85 hours of information from Jeffery Combs and his guest speakers, this is your ULTIMATE Empowering training library! Owning the complete Mastermind Library is a must for anyone serious about building their enterprise!

8-CD Audio Series $99.00 Value	8-CD Audio Series $99.00 Value	10-CD Audio Series $149.00 Value	8-CD Audio Series $99.00 Value	8-CD Audio Series $99.00 Value

8-CD Audio Series $99.00 Value	8-CD Audio Series $99.00 Value	8-CD Audio Series $99.00 Value	8-CD Audio Series $99.00 Value	8-CD Audio Series $99.00 Value

Single Audio CD $15.00 Value	Single Audio CD $15.00 Value	Single Audio CD $15.00 Value

Book $14.95 Value	Book $17.95 Value	Book $17.95 Value	Book $17.95 Value

Total Retail Value Exceeds $ 1, 200.00! • Special Discounted Offer Only $399.00 + S&H!
Toll Free: 800-595-6632

www.GoldenMastermind.com

New From Jeffery Combs!

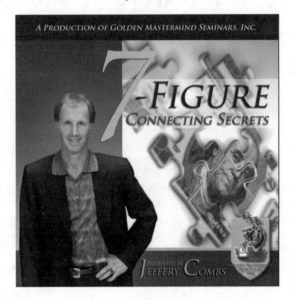

7-Figure Connecting Secrets Revealed!

Are you ready to create 7-figure income results in your enterprise? Successful careers are launched and fueled by skillfully created connections and you will be amazed when you discover how easy connecting really is! In this CD Jeffery Combs shares the simple skills he uses over and over to create connections with people in life and in business to consistently achieve 7-figure income results.

1. Develop Opportunity Seeking Perception
2. Ask Quality Questions
3. Listen and Receive
4. Ask for Referrals
5. Use Your Network
6. Listen to Your Intuition
7. Attract Great Connectors

Only Available Online at
www.GoldenMastermind.com

What Is the Secret to Success in Free Enterprise? Prospecting!!!

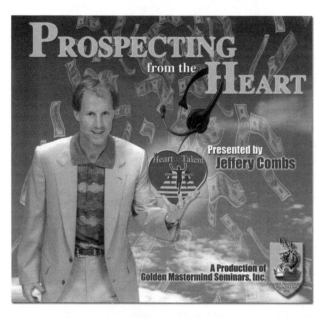

In this signature 8-CD audio program, Jeffery Combs reveals his secrets to creating multiple 7-figure income results and teaches you how to implement the same skills and strategies he uses each and every day to create the results you desire in your enterprise. The information in this program is designed to assist you to create internal transformations so you can prospect and connect effortlessly from your heart!

- Releasing Prospecting Anxiety
- Mastering the Inner Game of Selling
- Developing 7-Figure Habits to Create 7-Figure Results
- In the Moment Connecting
- Learn to Interview, Not Interrogate
- Setting Successful Appointments
- Releasing Rejection Once and for All

Prospecting is easy and fun when you understand the psychology of people. If you are ready to create financial success, you absolutely deserve to receive the insights Jeffery shares in Prospecting From The Heart!

www.GoldenMastermind.com

More Heart Than Talent
by Jeffery Combs

"Listen to him, learn what he says and live his wise, brilliant advice.
It will make your life infinitely better."
- Mark Victor Hansen
The Power of Focus and Co-Creator of Chicken Soup for the Soul

This Book Will Assist You to:

- Step Out of Your Talent and Into Your Heart
- Become The Leader Other People Are Looking For
- Become a Goal Getter, Not a Goal Setter
- Develop an Agenda for Change
- Understand Why You Do What You Do
- Glide Through Adversity
- Manage Yourself Instead of Your Time
- Develop Your Emotional Resilience
- Get Off the Emotional Roller Coaster!
- Live in Your Intuition
- Feel From Your Heart
- Be In The Moment

"On the journey to success, heart beats talent every time!"
- Jeffery Combs

Now Available at
www.BarnesandNoble.com
www.Amazon.com

MONEY IS MY FRIEND
FOR THE NEW MILLENNIUM

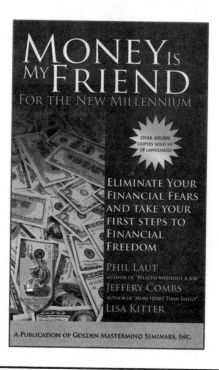

This Book Will Assist You to:

- Release the Common Causes of Poverty Consciousness
- The Benefits of Your Own Business
- How to Develop a Prosperity Mindset
- Couples and Money
- The Investing Law
- Improving Sales Results

Attracting and receiving money doesn't have to be a struggle! Learn tried and true methods for ending your love/hate relationship with money. The issues that confound your progress are more easily cured that endured with the methods in this book!

Now Available at
www.BarnesandNoble.com
www.Amazon.com

WOMEN IN POWER

A WOMAN'S GUIDE TO FREE ENTERPRISE

BY ERICA COMBS

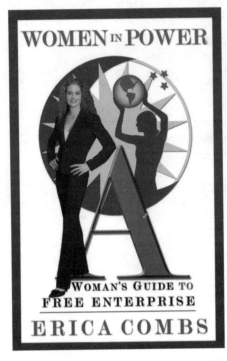

If you are ready to have free enterprise free you financially, emotionally and spiritually read my friend Erica's brilliant new book."

– Mark Victor Hansen
Co-creator, #1 New York Times best selling series
Chicken Soup for the Soul ®
Co-author, Cracking the Millionaire Code and The One
Minute Millionaire

Erica Combs is a woman who knows her power. Her creativity, talent and heart will assist you to achieve the success you seek.

- Jim Rohn
America's Foremost Business Philosopher

Whether you are already a successful entrepreneur, just beginning a new venture or simply romancing the vision of owning your own business one day, this book will greatly assist you to understand how to win the game of free enterprise.

Success will require that you begin to examine your current beliefs and give yourself permission to release those which no longer serve you so that you may adopt new and empowering beliefs to lead you to manifesting your dreams.

The purpose of this book is to create a foundation for you to begin your journey to personal power, and to create an anchor you can use to reconnect with your internal peace as you continue your journey of personal development in the land of free enterprise!

www.GoldenMastermind.com

BREAKTHROUGHS TO SUCCESS

A 2½ Day Intensive Personal Growth &
Entrepreneurial Retreat Featuring Jeffery & Erica Combs
Location: Stockton, CA

Breakthroughs Exercises:

- The Psychology of Wealth
- Letting Go of Your Ego!
- Emotional Healing
- Getting Money Right Emotionally
- Forgiveness
- Being in the Moment

Breakthroughs To Success will assist you to breakthrough and heal the emotional barriers that have kept you from achieving the level of success you deserve in your enterprise. Spend 2½ empowering days with Jeffery & Erica Combs in a small, private setting.

Receive luxury transportation to and from the Sacramento airport via limousine service, catered lunches, and hands-on training with Jeff & Erica!

Release Your Limitations & Discover The Power of Belief!

YOU DESERVE TO HAVE IT ALL!

800-595-6632
www.GoldenMastermind.com

GOLDEN MASTERMIND SEMINARS, INC.
6507 Pacific Ave. Suite 329 Stockton, CA 95207
Phone: 800-595-6632 • Fax: 209-467-3260
E-mail: GMS@GoldenMastermind.com
Website: www.GoldenMastermind.com

More Heart Than Talent Workshops

Are You Looking to Breakthrough Barriers in Your Life?
Don't Go It Alone!!!
Internationally Recognized Speaker, Success Coach, Author
and 7 Figure Income Earner Jeffery Combs
Brings "More Heart Than Talent" to a City Near You!
For Event Dates and Locations
Please Visit www.GoldenMastermind.com
Or Contact Us Toll Free: 800-595-6632

Topics & Exercises:

• More Heart Than Talent
• Being In the Moment
• Connecting Heart-to-Heart Exercise
• Getting Money Right Emotionally
• Your 10 Moments of Brillianc e

Jeffery Combs, the President of Golden Mastermind Seminars, Inc., is an Internationally Recognized Speaker, Author, and Trainer, and has Personally Coached Over 1,000 Individuals Worldwide. His Training Revolves Around Personal Growth and Development, Cuts to the Chase, and Delivers Information That Makes an Immediate Impact on Your Success! During This Special Workshop, Jeff Will be Conducting a Special In-depth Presentation on Projecting Success From Your Heart, Getting Money Right Emotionally, and Living Life "In The Moment"!

For Event Dates & Locations or to Reserve Seats ForYou & Your Team
Contact **Golden Mastermind Seminars, Inc.**
Phone: 800-595-6632 • Fax: 209-467-3260
Email: GMS@GoldenMastermind.com

YOU DESERVE TO BE THERE!